Melancthon Woolsey Stryker

**Hamilton, Lincoln, & other addresses**

Melancthon Woolsey Stryker

**Hamilton, Lincoln, & other addresses**

ISBN/EAN: 9783743328792

Manufactured in Europe, USA, Canada, Australia, Japa

Cover: Foto ©ninafisch / pixelio.de

Manufactured and distributed by brebook publishing software (www.brebook.com)

Melancthon Woolsey Stryker

**Hamilton, Lincoln, & other addresses**

# ADDRESSES
## OF
# MELANCTHON WOOLSEY STRYKER

# Hamilton Lincoln & other addresses

*BY*

MELANCTHON WOOLSEY STRYKER

*President of Hamilton College*

Utica, N. Y.
William T. Smith & Company
1896

Copyright, 1896, by
M. Woolsey Stryker.

*All rights reserved.*

## PUBLISHER'S NOTE

THIS volume gathers the chief Orations and Addresses, together with three Baccalaureate Sermons, given by President Stryker during three and a half years, beginning with 1893. A few of them are reprinted from public reports, and are given with the bracketed comments of their auditors, in the belief that this reflects in a not unacceptable way the color of their several occasions.

## CONTENTS

PAGE

I. ALEXANDER HAMILTON: An address before the Hamilton Club of Brooklyn, N. Y., January 11, 1895 . . . . . . . 9

II. ABRAHAM LINCOLN: An address before the Union League Club of Brooklyn, N. Y., February 12, 1895 . . . . . . . . . 25

III. OUR PURITAN FORBEARS: An address before the New England Society of New York City, December 22, 1893 . . . . 36

IV. THE DUTY OF ENTHUSIASM: An address at the Woodstock, Conn., celebration, July 4, 1894 . . . . . . . . . . . . 48

V. THE FUTURE OF THE INDEPENDENT COLLEGE: A paper read at the Convention of Colleges and Schools, at the Johns Hopkins University, at Baltimore, Md., December 1, 1894 . 59

VI. EMMA WILLARD: An address at the presentation of the RUSSELL SAGE Hall, at Troy, N. Y., May 16, 1895 . . . . 67

VII. IDEALS: An address before the graduates of the BARTHOLOMEW School, Cincinnati, Ohio, May 30, 1895 . . . . . . . 74

VIII. THE STEWARDSHIP OF KNOWLEDGE: An address at the opening of the Brooklyn Institute, September 30, 1895 . . . 92

IX. ETHICS IN POLITICS: A speech at the 127th Banquet of the Chamber of Commerce, New York City, November 19, 1895 . 102

X. SEEING THE UNSEEN: The baccalaureate sermon to the graduating class of '93, at Hamilton College, Sunday, June 18, 1893 . 112

XI. THE INDISSOLUBLE LIFE: The baccalaureate sermon to the class of '94, Hamilton College, June 24, 1894 . . . . . . . 126

## CONTENTS

XII. RADICAL AND CONSERVATIVE: The baccalaureate sermon to the class of '95, Hamilton College, June 23, 1895 . . . . . 138

XIII. CREEDS: The annual sermon before the Alumni of Auburn Theological Seminary, May 9, 1895 . . . . . . . . . . 152

XIV. PARTISANSHIP AND PATRIOTISM: A speech at the 'Hardware Dinner,' New York City, February 20, 1896 . . . . . . . 168

XV. THE DISTINCTIVE FUNCTION OF THE COLLEGE: Remarks before the University Club of Buffalo, N. Y., March 3, 1896 . . 180

# Alexander Hamilton

## AN ADDRESS DELIVERED BEFORE THE HAMILTON CLUB OF BROOKLYN
## JANUARY 11, 1895

---

*Mr. President and Gentlemen of the Hamilton Club*—Let me begin with grateful acknowledgment, both of the honor which you have conferred in asking me to speak to you on this anniversary and of your hearty and encouraging greeting. Let me also moderate all expectation by telling you that I am not the adept this occasion merits, but the merest novice at this festal art and withal let me confide, (tho my present presumption seems to contradict me), a modest one. Modest one must be facing such a theme and company—a company to which the details and suggestions of the theme are so familiar and which contains so many speakers of renowned power. You have heard of the good woman who prayed that her minister might be "anointed with the ile of Patmos!" [Laughter.] For many reasons too humorous to mention, I must bespeak, and, too, in your own behalf, your present entreaties for me. I am, alas, like the man who said he could "risk anything except temptation," and I freely confess that my good resolutions to talk less and think more, to have more bung and less spigot, were quite vanquished by the tempting opportunity to stand here as the representative, however poorly, of an interest which holds in reverence that name which is its title, as it is also the title of this group. In a recent most courteous note relating to this evening, your president graciously assured me that you "recognize very distinctively the patronymic relationship of the club and the college." It is indeed a broad common ground and well may we each attempt untiringly to maintain the spirit of Alexander Hamilon and to recognize our debt to his superlative services. But this duty is not elective and singular, it goes with our birthright as loyal Americans. If to that duty we are, *e nomine*, peculiarly and publicly pledged, it is also one shared joyfully by all citizens of this land who are intelligent in its constitutional history. [Applause.] For his great name is not one merely to grace a holiday, but it is woven into the very texture of our chief events. All that is subsequent to him is like a palimpsest above his original script. His initials are the watermark under every page. If any meager recitation of mine shall be effective to stimulate your mental energy — if I can but start your thinking by a kind of flying switch — I shall be satisfied; for a train of treasure is far more than the wheezy engine that moves it. Should I seem parsimonious of ideas, remember that I have now given you the oars and that I only agree to do the steering while you row.

It was ninety years ago that the heavy-booming guns at the Battery were answered by the French and English warships then in the harbor yonder, and that to their miserere — the three nations to which he was related joining in that last salute — the heart of the people of his fond adoption quivered in responsive pain. So, in Trinity Churchyard, close by the middle of its south wall, where today a quaint and time-worn construction of stone with its obscuring inscription but poorly marks his sepulture, they laid all of him that could die, to

> "Let the sound of those he wrought for,
> And the feet of those he fought for,
> Echo round his bones forever more."

There was no Tennyson to celebrate in majestic ode "an empire's lamentations," and sooth it was but a little empire then and this great city but a trivial village: but time and "the strength of a diffusive thought" have wrought the poem, and his mausoleum is a mighty dome upheld by well-nigh fifty pillars. That little provincial New York is now, as a centre of

## HIS PRECOCITY

metropolitan population, the second on Earth. He sleeps well,

> "While the stars burn, the moons increase,
> And the great ages onward roll."

To him and to ourselves and to those who shall follow we owe it more strenuously to consider our immortal debt to one who so heroically endured "as seeing the invisible." The outline that dates furnish, however familiar to you, it will be well rapidly to trace. Hamilton was born on this day, 1757, in the small island of Nevis, his father and his name utterly Scotch and his mother of Huguenot lineage. So in his veins blended the stuff of the race of Knox and of the race of Coligny and Beza. At 12 a counting-house of Santa Cruz had in him a clerk of exceptional facility and of premature commercial tact. Already he was of manly force and trustiness. At 15 here — not long to be a stranger — and busy with books at Elizabeth, N. J. At 16 an eager student advancing rapidly in King's College, whose title by his good help was soon and thereafter to be Columbia. What a star is that which stands by his name upon the roll of that venerable school to which your own club has given its present great president! At 17 he began and with no 'prentice hand threw himself upon the issue as a speaker and a pamphleteer. At 19 captain of artillery, maneuvering his stubborn guns with skill at Harlem and White-Plains. At 20 upon the staff of the commander-in-chief with rank of lieutenant-colonel. At 23 he weds Eliza, daughter of General Schuyler. As lieutenant-colonel of infantry he led one of the last charges upon Cornwallis' works at Yorktown. He sits in Congress 1782-83 and again 1787-88, in which last period he becomes the controlling spirit of the Constitutional Convention. Two-thirds of the substance of that sagacious exposition which we call "The Federalist" was Hamilton's critical contribution toward the ratification of the Convention's work. Well has it been called the "Bible of Republicanism." In 1780, at the age of 32, as Washington's "principal and most trusted friend," he became the first Secretary of the Treasury.

In 1708 he was made Inspector-General of the army, and in 1799 Commander-in-Chief. In 1800 he was president-general of the Society of the Cincinnati. In 1804, Burr, largely thro the influence of Hamilton (who read him well and distrusted his sinister ambition), being defeated in his effort to become Governor of New York, sought a quarrel with him. Hamilton accepted the cartel and fell — murdered. It was July 11, and on the next day at the age of 47 he died. So ended his crowded career of nearly thirty years of public service. "That is not a common chance that takes away a noble mind," and the personal traits of such a phenomenal man claim the most careful pondering.

Those traits were rare, one by one, and in their combination they were marvelous. Much, of course, he owed to natal gifts, much to the variety of his early training, much to the emergencies that influenced his most flexible years, much to his prompt consorting with the ablest men: but heredity, impulse, circumstance, occasion and environment illustrate — they do not explain. He was what he was. All else defines, this isolates. From the first Hamilton was avid of large things, and, hating abstractions, he sought broad ideas in order to their concrete and constructive uses. His faith in primary principles was tirelessly industrious to search out and establish these: but his prescience was never ministrant to that vanity which often pretends to evince originality as if independent of dire mental toil. He forewent no labor of self-equipment, but, mixing all he did with brains, and with no occult reserve of method, he steered for conviction and hesitated neither for odium nor for applause. It was this rectilinear purpose, this undeviating candor, that both made him to be immensely loved, and, by indirect, subtle and plausible minds, as intensely hated. In either sense his way was straightway. If he lacked, it was in conciliation and patience. Precocity is not of itself a virtue; it may even be a defect; it is always a peril. It was in spite of his youth, and not because of it, that he was so early heeded and followed, for with all his energy of enthusiasm he seemed endowed at the beginning with the fertile resource and balanced judgment of middle life. That gallant, expressive face not only glowed with heat, but also beamed with light. That lithe, supple and animated form spoke of command as well as of impulse. Well for us that in him the range of hope had not time to be cramped by that incertitude which so often poses as discretion. [Applause.] Well for us that he so trusted himself to truth, and that his early disciplines had made him both so rapid and so exact. It was thus he seized hours at which looser-girded wills faltered or shrank. His promptness rivalled occasion, and serried obstinacy yielded to his intrepid assaults. [Applause.] It was not his own success he sought, but the triumph of a mighty cause. Had he preferred power, which is transient, to influence, which endures; had he been a partisan rather than a patriot, a self-seeker rather than the trustee of a future beyond even his hope or ken; had he been duplex, where he was open, lucid and sincere; then he had not impressed his individuality upon a whole America as the truest translator of her predestinate nationality. When the surrender was making at Yorktown it is said that some of the American troops began to cheer. "Silence," ordered Washington, "let posterity cheer for us." They are not always happiest, but they are always blessedest who prefer faith to popularity, and who appeal from the plaudits of an hour to the solemn vindications of history. There this great jurist rested his great case. He was neither sophist nor paralogist. He dwelt above manipulation, and compromise, and expedient, and formula, and all mere passport. He sought the underlying principles and the ultimate reality. His soul went into his plea. With warmth and grace, but with a peculiar logical simplicity—a clearness that became clarity—and with the unshaken courage of one compelled by conviction, he summoned his facts and marshalled his reasons. His was the strategy of unambushed truth and the elastic energy of a direct will. [Cheers.] The power of the will in oratory is elemental. An orator is a leader—a captain and captor of men—his captaincy is captivation; for hearts are made that way. But the genius for this control is none other than undisguised and uncalculating devotion to a cause. The words of such an one are spermatic. To him the souls of men respond as tinder kisses flame. It was said that in the convention of '88 Hamilton "converted his opponents on his feet," and later still his impressiveness had no dubious tribute when Congress refused to hear him as Secretary of the Treasury, lest it should be too much convinced. But he was no theatrical rhapsodist. His rhetoric served, not mastered, his syllogism. With pen, as with voice, he was a chief of assemblies. He was a sharp sword and two-edged. He was the exponent and champion of frank and fearless argument. Malignity might vituperate, but he did not pause. Malice might misrepresent him, but he never sulked. Cunning was not in him, nor little envy, nor treachery. He met each new issue as it arose, and, his enemies themselves being judges, he was never put to the worse in free and open encounter. Nor were his strokes sporadic or inconsecutive. He stayed well. At Philadelphia he thralled his auditors thro a speech of six hours, and at each point of controversy thro all those momentous sessions he was armed and alert. Never did he for one repulse forego his purpose. Continuity was his secret. He sought to show the symmetry of that which he beheld and was glad that "from Discussion's lips" it should be

"Set in all lights by many minds
To bind the interest of all." [Applause.]

"The noble and magnificent perspective of a great federal republic" filled his eyes, and he, too, was not disobedient unto the heavenly vision. Life, fortune, honor were to that sacredly rendered, ungrudgingly, unweariedly, unregrettingly, and, thank God, with absolute success. *He had no secrets from his country!* [Cries of "Bravo!"] To the versatility, the acumen, the deep symmetrical strength of this rare being all witnesses agree. Morris, Kent, Story, Marshall (by both direct tribute and judicial decisions), Von Holst, and a hundred more exalt his work. Bryce says: "He stands in the front rank of a generation never surpassed in history." For remember the eighteenth cycle, if you would be just to it, not by its moribund first seventy years, but by the tragic awakenings of its last quarter. Guizot said: "He powerfully contributed to secure to the constitution its every element of order, force and duration." Talleyrand said that he "never knew his equal." "He has divined Europe." And what schoolboy does not know Webster's sonorous acclaim? "He smote the rock of national resources and the waters gushed forth. He touched the corpse of national credit and it sprang to its feet." For my part, I venture especially to affirm Hamilton's rare magnanimity. In a day of reckless political envy he, with Washington, shines exceptional. Adams, Jefferson, Madison, Monroe, make this excellence of his vivid by contrast. When I meditate the deep damnation of his taking-off, it is piteous to recall that but a little earlier he had upon entreaty made a private loan to the dastard who slew him. Of all those federalists who

> "Wrought in a sad sincerity,
> And builded better than they knew,"

Hamilton is in the van.

It was he who had made Webster's best possible, and his worst impossible. It was Hamilton's spirit that replied to Hayne. It was Hamilton's spirit that spoke thro Jackson's lips to the nullifiers, and, alas, the lack of it that succumbed to the devious and disastrous compromise that followed. It was Hamilton's soul that made way for Lincoln and for liberty. We dwell, gentlemen, under the roof he fastened, and which of us will not, with his heart in his throat, remember the legacy of that leader of leaders, and say with a gratitude that is also a vow, "I, too, am a Federalist." [Applause.] Let me turn you rapidly toward some of the memorials of his commanding fame, whose spirit reigns here tonight, and so approach the swift review of that greatest result which is his pre-eminence and crown. And let me diverge somewhat from the historical order to seek the poetical. At the base of all the public miseries succeeding the peace of '83 lay poverty — poverty and with it apathy. Productive industry frightened and unprotected, credit prostrate, the army muttering, intense localism breeding the maggots of secession, quivering and perilous unrest, universal faction, Congress discordant and impotent. It was a needful discipline. It prepared the way for that recognition of unity of interest which alone could supersede the baleful and portentous distress. While Europe sneered at us, and the stoutest hearts shrank before calamities that threatened cataclysm, Hamilton, as the first secretary of the treasureless treasury, addressed to the situation his whole intellect. Much was chaotic and all was new. Against these somber skies this mentor of the first administration towered alone. Upon his commanding wisdom was laid the whole and fundamental problem of finance. The ship of state, such as it was, no lofty frigate then, but a water-logged schooner rather, plunged and rolled amid cross currents and upon a lee shore. The crew was spent and all but mutinous. "Sauve qui peut," was a gaining cry. It was this indomitable pilot who brought the craft thro the perils of great waters and safe to port. Foreign censors stood amazed as Hamilton set fast our public credit upon the eternal rock of honesty. Woe betide the hand that would unwrite his work, and that would, printing a counterfeit presentment of Liberty upon fifty-one cents' worth of silver, invite credulity "to trust in God" for the other forty-nine! [Loud cheers.] No; true faith in God involves good faith toward men. The philosophy of fiat currency—be it of paper or of pewter—leads to a maudlin ethics, and horrors untold lie that way. The eighth commandment is not to be repealed, even for silly Americans. Nothing comes so dear at last as cheap money, and they who urge it would worst rob the least able; for the fewer dollars a man has the more need that they be of the very best in all the markets of the world. We do not yet want to be an *argentine* republic. Nor can sectionalism in finance live long, putting, as it does, a penalty upon that capital which is the surest friend of the craftsman. [Applause.] The hand of Hamilton traced the outline and wrought out the whole detail of a system whose soundness was proven in its success and stability. Revenue, currency, a funded debt, the mint, the bank, were creations of a skill that fathomed both needs and resources. West Point was Hamilton's idea. His forecast planned for and frustrated the imminent war with France. The so-called Monroe doctrine was but a plagiarism of Hamilton's proclamation of neutrality. The exalted patriotism and still pertinent admonitions of Washington's farewell address were submitted to and touched by the pen that he so long had trusted without disappointment.

And now, with apology, I advert to that college sitting at the very core of this imperial State and binding about her brow, as a chaplet, that name which tonight you delight to honor. Kirkland, the great Indian lover, was patriot, too, and army chaplain at Fort Stanwix. Hamilton knew him well and advised with and assisted the missionary's hope to plant, under "the smiles of the God of wisdom," a true school upon the far frontiers. As an active member of that Board of Regents whose comprehensive idea so well fitted his synthetic temper— (that Board whose present chancellor is one of our college's most honored sons, and one of whose most distinguished members, my friend, Dr. McKelway, will address you tonight) —Hamilton was chosen as chief sponsor and became the first charter applicant and trustee of the academy which rapidly grew into the college. Steuben laid the corner stone in 1794. Have we not good right with such associations proudly to wear as our distinctive colors the Continental blue and buff? We cherish that history and would honor it. For more than thirty years our commencements have heard a competitive prize oration upon some feature of the work of New York's foremost son. With this goes also a parallel oration "The Duties of Educated Young Men to the State." Is it any wonder that from that high hilltop 183 men—with General Hawley among them—went down to the great war to maintain the doctrines of the Federalist? That was one for every six of the sons then born to us. [Applause.] Is it any wonder that Dr. Elihu Root sat in a group of nine who love that old campus, at the very centre of the tasks of the New York Constitutional Convention of last summer, and who well paid the interest (if any was in arrears) upon that old charter of 1793? [Cheers.] Some things go by avoirdupois, but Alexander Hamilton is to be taken by Troy weight. When I reckon patriotism, eloquence, effectiveness, I am well content to be an alumnus of a little college of large men. And, by the way, when some day Brooklyn is making her last will and testament and all your treasures are bequeathing, remember that I now put in a plea for that noble statue which guards and glorifies your doors. What a figure of speech it is, and with what difficnlty I have carried past it that most brittle tenth commandment! I fear if it were more portable, that nothing short of force would replevin it from beneath those swinging elms where it ought to stand. [Applause.] That ardent attitude recalls the scenes at Poughkeepsie. With all his soul he pleaded and by a majority so small that one shivers to recall the parliamentary chances, he won, and was the father of the Constitution. It was no still-birth, but alive. What a voice it had, and what a child it is, to be sure, this year of grace 1895—its benignant and penetrating eyes still bright with youth and liberty. But it was born, as every man-child is born, in anguish.

> "For all the past of time reveals
> A bridal dawn of thunder peals,
> When truth hath wedded fact." [Applause.]

Thirteen distinct and various sovereignties, wrangling, greedy, stubborn, could not long cohere under an arrangement which was at best of provisional utility, and which Washington described as "a shadow without a substance." "If the federal government should lose its authority civil war would certainly follow," was Hamilton's prediction. But that authority would be lost unless vitally strengthened. He saw the menace and reading the analogy of dead republics prepared with astute decision to parry it. Rivalry meant ruin, sympathy meant strength. The coalition of fragments must be changed into "a solid coercive union." No mere treaty alliance would do. That was, as Madison said, " imbecile, discordant, precarious." The idea of confederacy had shown itself incapable to realize that community of life — that latent, but crescent, sense of nationality which was the inward voice of America's providential calling. Germany and Italy, thro their long and painful gestations, afford us similar instances of the inadequacy of the confederation theory to affirm the mission of a homogeneous people. That theory is over-centrifugal. Our revolution, whose success is one of the marvels, almost miracles, of history, had wakened an instinct, but the years of process were still necessary to show out the disintegrating elements of a selfish, vacillating and irascible colonialism. Like the twins in the womb of Rebekah the old divisive spirit struggled with the new cohesive spirit. Esau came first, but the nobler offspring was the later and it was revealed "the elder shall serve the younger." The national idea was growing. The very word "continental" was significant. "We, the people" ran the declaration. [Applause.] The constitution was an interpretation of a life anterior to itself. The instrument was the demonstration of prior fact. Geography and history blended to affirm this destiny of wedlock. Many stars, one constellation—"an indestructible union of indestructible states"— toward that we tended and to that we came. Well writes Mulford, in that great treatise of his on the Nation — "There has been in the history of no people the witness to a higher unity." But eyes were dull then. The body was suffering with its schismatical parts. In the spirit of sectionalism which is essential disunion, province was saying to province — "I have no need of thee." Perverse local interests were ready to write severalty where God had written commonalty. The wonder

is that any hand could stroke those angry seas into rhythm.
[Cheers.] When we recall the reluctance, not only of the Carolinas, but of selfish Massachusetts, cranky Rhode Island and greedy New York, and recall the slender margin by which all this insularity was overcome, we may well tremble and praise. Hamilton never bated a jot of his purpose. By every tireless resource he explained, advocated, appealed. The sequel vindicates him. The present Empire State is the reply to the dismal forebodings of those then in it who assailed his work. In the light of events he stands forth as the one great prophet amid a throng of doleful prognosticators. That mighty sum in complex fractions was done—Hamilton had brought them to a common denominator. First came dear little Delaware, the "blue hen" with her chickens, and may she never be degraded by electing corrupt men to her places of honor! [Applause.] Last came Rhode Island—all in, and the ark floated. The constitution was a happy mean between confederacy on the one hand and imperialism on the other. The structure of the Senate, which only rash impatience undervalues, illustrates the counterpoise of the system. That a framework of government, so flexible yet so firm, and with so much that was experimental, could be made *de novo*, is the wonder of political philosophy. Hamilton was accused of monarchial tendencies because he distrusted the tyranny of an unmixed democracy. But he only appealed to the restraints of that second sense which ought to triumph over extempore impulse. If you will pardon the anachronism, I will say that it was air-break offsetting steam-chest—popular power working in both and in balance—safety complementing speed. The Senate, with its check upon the haste of untried majorities, says Think twice. [Loud applause.] They tell us that Hamilton was aristocratical. In the good and accurate sense he was that, but not in the sense of promoting oligarchy. He longed to have a government by the best. Who does not? [Cheers.] If we have made of his electoral college an elaborate *cui bono*, that may show him to have been too sanguine of his political heirs, it does not prove

his theory to have been wrong. Fending alike the dangers from the *imperium* and the *vulgus*, from scented pride and unsoaped envy, he steered by the middle channel. Our troubles have not been from the chart, but from the crew! The white of an egg and the venom of a rattlesnake are both albumen. The difference between food and poison is a matter of slight chemical proportion. The revolution was a mighty evolution. It was at last perceived to have been a struggle for English liberties, too; that Burke and Chatham were right, and the fatuous Lord North and the fat-witted George III. were wrong. We had fought the good fight of a man against prerogative, as we fought again for labor as against caste. That was true, even if Mr. Gladstone, the great tide-waiter of the nineteenth century [applause and laughter], could not see it; even if that licensed and fascinating scold Carlyle did interpret the roar and smoke of our civil war as "the burning out of an old chimney," and seemed not to care if the house went with it. John Bull whistled, but found his whistle a costly toy. So little do men perceive of where the point lies whose heads are thick with the wit of *Punch*. [Laughter and applause.] But the beginning was not the end, nor is the end yet, tho "now is our salvation nearer than when we first believed." The old factional elements gathered in partisan antagonism. It may be gravely doubted whether if that tortuous and temporizing reactionary, Thomas Jefferson, had not fortunately been absent in France his jealous weight would not have sufficed to "turn the poised and trembling scale" away from nationality. We moved in and began to live under the "new roof." Thenceon our history becomes an effort to realize both the Constitution and ourselves. Hamilton thought the Union "might endure thirty years"—how nearly did he divine the reach of the Virginia resolutions and the date of nullification!—but even he did not see that the instrument was an effect rather than a cause, that while it registered so much it subtended far more! It was a law; but the nation was a life. Great as were the specific bequests the residuum was far greater. The testators did not measure their legacy. They did not then know that they were bequeathing an estate, which some perfervid orator described as "bounded on the north by the aurora, on the east by the sunrise, on the south by the precession of the equinoxes, and on the west by the day of judgment!" [Cheers.]

For three-score years and ten, two principles, the centripetal and the centrifugal, were in collision, and making ready to grapple. Then, after that appointed labor and sorrow, the enduring knowledge that our orbit is an ellipse, with its two foci, both determinate and mutual. It was the school of pain: but it was God's! It was sharp surgery: but with a blessed end. The very being of this Union went into the crucible, and melted in the furnace of Antietam, and Shiloh, and Chickamauga, and the Wilderness. We, too, as all-American, will cherish the memory of the devoted, if mistaken, bravery of Albert Sidney Johnson and of Stonewall Jackson, and of his sword who was turned back from Round Top, while we repudiate the oligarchic fallacies of Toombs and Stephens. Where these failed let no feebler hands attempt. The cause of separation is a lost cause! The great replevin has been served! *I am a Federalist!* It is no vague theory. It affirms the solidarity, the common destiny, of a people. I am with Washington as against Jefferson, for John Jay as against George Clinton, for Webster as against Calhoun, for Lincoln as against Davis, for those two Southerners, Farragut and Thomas, against Lee; for Alexander Hamilton, as against that other, whose treacherous nature Hamilton so clearly discovered, and who with treason and murder upon his soul, went out from the vice-presidency as Aaron of old from the presence of the Lord—a leper. [Great applause.] The whole is both the sum of all its parts, and is itself greater than that sum. True patriotism is synthetic. I love best my duty to the whole. Those dreadful swaths of the dead were not reaped for nought! While the uncounted brave sleep on, and the constellations march west until the reveille of the archangel, let the survivors and heirs of that bitter time lock hands, and standing with blending cheers and tears above the buried armies, register an implacable oath that no bastard doctrine of unfraternity shall ever again assail our common hearthstone! And let history go for this at least, that the Constitution down to its latest amendment shall be best interpreted by its friends. [Applause.] We are called to meet the trials of a new age. Our expanding nation requires that, as by a pantagraph, old fundamental principles be extended to enlarged problems. This Union that we love is imperial in opportunity, therefore in duty. Ability is responsibility. By the grace of God responsibility is ability. What we ought, we can! Let us swear it—what we can, we will.

   So once as old Leonidas
     Held his, will we our bivouac,
   With daybreak crowd the narrow pass,
     And cram the droves of devils back.
   So, thundering down the thorofare,
     Against the odds and chaos rout,
   With lightning in his streaming hair,
     Blazed Sheridan! and "Right about,"
   With will that made the rebel writhe,
     The army's dulled edged whetting keen,
   Swung left, swung right, the loyal scythe,
     And mowed the Shenandoah clean!
   Spite of torpedoes in the bay,
     So Farragut, with steady keel,
   Up to close gunshot split the way,
     And set the stars above Mobile!
   And so, to bless the coming years,
     And in the faith of heaven born,
   We'll hail the call for volunteers;—
     For righteous hope was ne'er forlorn!
   Ah! 'tis time we were beginning
     To build our platforms to the rock;
   Smooth planks and rotten underpinning
     Can never bide the future's shock.
   So hew them rough, but hew them strong—
     Stout creeds mean burly deeds again—
   Trample the tom-tom and the gong,
     Cease worshipping the weather vane.
   Let low commercial special pleas,

>     With smiting knees, spell out their doom!
>   Ungag the great moralities,
>     Give clean men clean sweep with clean broom.
>   So shall a people's candidate
>     Again in spotless toga wait.
>   Out on the shuffled lying tissues!
>     What patriots mean, let parties say,
>   Confront the living, bleeding issues,
>     And do the deeds that dare today.  [Loud applause.]

No State bears the name of Hamilton, as none is yet named for Lincoln: but this Union of States, one endowment, one land, one history, one task, one flag, one God, is the deathless memorial of them both. I join their names and their service. Let it grow from more to more, as the ample fulfillment of them both — a realm of magnificent, because equal, laws, administered by fearless, because incorruptible, men. Until out of the calm eternities shall break the days of the Son of Man, let it be our unanimous prayer and our unshaken pledge, "Each of us for every other, and God for us all!" [Loud and long-continued applause.]

# Abraham Lincoln.

## AN ADDRESS DELIVERED BEFORE THE UNION LEAGUE CLUB OF BROOKLYN, FEBRUARY 12, 1895.

---

*Mr. President and Gentlemen*—It is time for an American Book of Days. The land we love is old enough and rich enough in men and achievements to have a rubricated record all its own.

The dates which punctuate its great events, its births and burials, its successive and interwoven crises of national evolution, its high tides and low, its "storms and tempests greater than almanacs can report," its feasts and fasts, its anguish and its anthems—these dates make a calendar with all its weeks illuminated and emphatic. More than we often pause to remember are we rich in history, not of a continental, but of a world-wide significance. Our life is of inter-centurial and planetary import. Each month is a volume, with its peculiar, illustrious and garlanded events. Wonder at all that our Aprils have witnessed, recall the annals of our great Julys, and then, you who love your country and treasure in your hearts her excellences of character and action—her sins, her repentances, her renewed probations—turn your thoughts to February, least in length of the twelve, but with two natal days, star-set and resplendent, and own the month that has such a 22d and such a 12th, the chief and brightest in all the round of the zodiac!

We are met, under the compulsions of a common reverence, to keep high festival, upon one of Columbia's cradle-nights, nay, to recall the gift, thro us, of one of the royal heirs of a world's admiration and affection. Ours indeed he is: but not ours only. The pantheon of Time claims him as one of Humanity's types and leaders. The "razure of oblivion" shall never touch his story, nor devotion to its high import become obsolete.

Amid the awed and woful group that watched that wild April night sink to the ashen dawn, Stanton was one, and when all was ended, it was his voice that spake out in solemn and befitting prophecy, "Now he belongs to the ages." The ages claim him. Thenceforward no one city, commonwealth or clime could appropriate him. History admits no transient and local monopoly to intrude between her and her elect dead. They are her own. She is their Rizpah and their Rachel.

"Never before that startled morning"—(wrote Lowell, at the conclusion of that essay whose strong and chiseled paragraphs go with the masculine emotion of his commemoration ode to make up his complete and unsurpassed tribute)— "Never before that startled morning did such multitudes of men shed tears for one they had never seen. Never was funeral panegyric so eloquent as the silent look of sympathy which strangers exchanged when they met on that day. Their common manhood had lost a kinsman."

That day is one of the strange indelible memories of my boyhood. How long and how little seems this interval of thirty years! But as each year has gone, with what certainty of just conviction, it has added one more tier to the masonry whereon is founded that ascendant and invulnerable fame. How such a story effaces the poor pride of language! How unequal are iridescent word-bubbles to catch and carry the tremulous half-lights and the true splendors of that luminiferous character! How must the soul stammer and sob that yields to the whole appeal of a spirit so great, so genuine, so gentle. Little indeed will the world heed, nor long remember, what any lips can now say of him,— enough that it will never forget what he did for us and for all men.

Who, then, shall presume to think that he has well summarized or at all completely analyzed the contents of such a life?

I lay my withering blossoms with those of his innumerable lovers, knowing that were their stems of gold and their petals of ruby, these would rust and dim long before the tooth of time had touched his immortal renown. I deprecate your heed to me, even while I entreat it. Think round, past, over, beyond, my frail and slender utterances. Let your reasoned gratitude and heartfelt admiration weave their own tributes in words that no man can utter. Let the "mystic chords" that he knew so well to touch into music, sound their master's requiem. *Sursum Corda!* He was God's gracious gift to a tormented and distracted time. He took who gave. He who gave and took, guards the inaccessible honor of a supreme and solitary soul, who, "having served his generation by the will of God, fell on sleep."

Bare-browed and wet-eyed, we stand in this our day under a firmament whose four-and-forty stars, unnamed and indistinguishable by any claim of severalty, make one unrivalled and unquenchable constellation, and highly resolve that Abraham Lincoln shall not have lived in vain nor vainly died!

And we declare our faith that the theme of that lost leader's greatness will still be new, curious, alluring, inspiring, until America shall have failed of her memory, until patriotism is senile, until self-sacrifice is no longer cogent, until popular government is moribund and democracy is numbered with the lost arts.

In the city of Chicago, at the entrance of the beautiful park that bears his name, there is placed commandingly, a statue of our greatest President.

Doubtless nearly all of you are familiar with its noble and unassuming pose. But what has always most impressed my imagination is that which stands just behind the exalted figure of the man — the empty chair! Never was vacant throne so suggestive and so full. Well might those words have been sculptured there which Lincoln uttered so early as 1858 — "Tho I now sink out of view, I believe I have made some marks which will tell for the cause of liberty long after I am gone." All of the memorials of such a nature and the reminiscences of such a life are significant and inestimably precious. We are to be glad that the narrative by his partner, Herndon, both establishes so much intimate fact and dispels so much possible myth. It was an unusual witticism of Longfellow's that auto-biography is what biography ought to be! This close friend more than any other, or than all others, sets forth the real personality without gloss or apology. We want the negative to be untouched in a single line, that we may get the truest impression of one who sat, quite behind what any strange or casual eye could see, within a most sensitive reticence. Frank as Lincoln was, inaustere, accessible — there was an inwardness and reserve behind whose further curtains few penetrated, and they but seldom. It is in his public words that we receive the deepest revelations of that strong and longing soul, so tender and so taciturn. His phenomenal gift of narrative was the alleviation not the assertion of his inmost self. Talk was his refuge from a proud and stately sorrow, a most pathetic and melancholy reverie. He was born under the sign of Aquarius. His life was clouded and rainy. Some of the sweetest sources of happiness were frozen to him. His yearning spirit turned upon itself and for the most part sealed its records. Upon that Cromwellian face (for tho it was more than Cromwell's, it was Cromwellian, wart and all) there were the seams of early responsibility and long restraint, and in all the humor of his smile there lurked the twitch of pain.

We all know the story of his early days — Kentucky, Indiana, Illinois — the bare poverty, the indomitable struggle to learn, the country law office with its rough clinic of human beings — its pathology of affairs, his small book lore and yet his keen literary susceptibility, that apparent listlessness in which he thought, and thought, and grew. All around, as we see it, what a wretched school, and yet what a schooling God gave him there! Soft raiment never sat well upon that home-spun king. Here, providentially, and out of the unlikeliest origins, was six feet and four inches of man. Little thripenny minds once sneered at his suburbanity and thought him outlandish, but splitting fencing or riving sophistry, steering a flatboat or a government, at the cabin hearth or at the capital of the Republic, in county law or commander of armies and fleets—that man, uncouth of limb and courtly of heart, is always and only Abraham Lincoln! There was but one, there will be no other, the mould is broken. "The case of that huge spirit is now cold."

Where did he get that aquiline wit, that shrewd and sensitive judgment, that pronged logic, that felicity of instance, that sure touch of nature, that vital and saline style? For, he was cunning in the niceties of language and coined wisdom into colloquial aphorism. What tough sense, what absence of vaporing, what conclusive directness, what sagacious transparency. "Honest Old Abe"—what a thirty-third degree of popular confidence was that! Which of us does not remember his wish that other generals "would get some whisky of the same kind"—his ballot-winning remark about "swapping horses while crossing a stream"—his appealling fun over "Uncle Sam's web feet." Thackeray, once for all, defined a snob as "one who admires mean things meanly." A great man is one who seeks great things in a great way. So was Lincoln great. He "never sold the truth to serve the hour."

With marvelous development he rose to each new demand and met it adequately, and there was never a day when he was not more of a man than the day before. Vast tact and absolute rectitude together. He was a student of occasion, but never in the shifty and selfish sense an opportunist. He discerned concrete issues and was no doctrinaire. He cared for results and was no respecter of persons. He used what he could get, and so got what he could use, knowing how to pursue that high expediency whose duty it is both to forego and to transcend mere legalitys. Astute in deliberation and biding his time, he never surrendered to others one ounce of his own responsibility, and proved his wisdom in taking all the advice he could get and using what he thought best.

"Gentle, plain, just and resolute," he surprised those who had thought to control him by his revelations of aptitude and of decision. Lowell wrote: "While dealing with unheard-of complications at home, he must soothe a hostile neutrality abroad, waiting only a pretext to become war." What tasks were these and with what untried tools! His temper equaled the emergency. He wielded war measures without flinching, yet always as an elect citizen, and so loved both the Union and the Constitution, that in their preservation he saved the one from those who would have destroyed it, and the other from those who would have defended it to death by quibbles. He saw that the Union was the very life of the Constitution — that academic distinctions are trivial in a struggle for existence — he could not consent to the cult of a disembodied spirit, nor protect the constitution of a corpse! His elastic tact was also stubborn. He refused to embroil us with angry England in the Trent affair, yet made the bully halt when thro the lips of Minister Adams he said: "It is unnecessary for me to remind your lordship that this means war!" Even to John Bull what "Hosea Bigelow" called "the fencin' stuff," seemed likely to come a little too high!

Lincoln's self-restraint was not that of "a being without parts and passions," but of one controlling his forces for use. Of slavery he said in '55: "I bite my lips and keep quie:t" but, a while later, stirred to the depths by the seizure of a free black boy at New Orleans, he said — and I take his indignation not as an oath but as a vow — "By God, gentlemen, I'll make the ground of this country too hot for the feet of slaves!" It was in that resolve that he entered upon the great debate in Illinois. He loved peace: but as a "just and lasting peace." "I hope it will come soon, and come to stay, and so come as to be worth the keeping for all future time." But his integrity never blenched. In the teeth of the counsels of timid friends he crystalized the truth in 1858. "This Union cannot endure, half slave and half free. A house divided against itself cannot stand." Withal, his rugged patience was as cautious, strategic, diplomatic, as it was persistent and courageous. Patience in him became a genius, a purpose that censors could neither hurry nor hinder.

> "He knew to bide his time;
> And can his fame abide
> Still patient, in his simple faith sublime,
> Till the wise years decide.
> Great captains with their guns and drums,
> Disturb our judgments for the hour:
> But at last silence comes.
> These all are gone, and, standing like a tower,
> Our children shall behold his fame;
> The kindly, earnest, brave, far-seeing man,
> Sagacious, patient, dreading praise, not blame,
> New birth of our new soil, the first American!"

This many-sided, yet directly simple President, this greatest Democrat of history, ennobled the people by trusting them and trusting himself to them, as they ennobled themselves by responding to that trust. "When he speaks," (wrote Lowell in 1864, in that monumental essay which I have before quoted) "it seems as if the people were listening to their own thinking aloud." His alert ear heard always that little click which precedes the striking of the clock. "It is most proper (he said at Buffalo) that I should wait and see the developments and get all the light possible, so that when I do speak authoritatively I may be as near right as possible." "Why should there not be (so went his first inaugural) a patient confidence in the ultimate justice of the people?" At "this great tribunal" he pleaded. "This is essentially a peoples' contest," ran his first message.

He knew how to interpret public opinion, and it answered him with a mighty and unbetrayed confidence. He both roused it to self-recognition and registered its vast resolve. The, to me, most moving lyric of those days utters that response of the nation, as the deed vindicated the song:

> "Six hundred thousand loyal men
> And true have gone before,
> And we're coming, Father Abraham,
> Three hundred thousand more!"

Verily he had prophesied well, in his good-by to the citizens of Indianapolis, "Of the people when they rise in mass in behalf of the union and liberties of their country, truly it may be said, 'The gates of hell shall not prevail against them.'"

This soul to whose noble abstraction and dedicated purpose the small gossip of the world was naught, drank deep the cup of vicarious pain. He paid daily the penalty of heroic love. In his sympathy he became a sacrifice. He "bore his cross" for the soldiers in the field and the mothers in their homes. And all the while he was "sustained and cheered by an unfaltering trust," a "faith that right makes might," "that in some way men can not see all will be well in the end." He deserves a place with "the elders who obtained a good report thro faith," and yet who only foresaw Canaan and the Christ to be. He came, like Moses, no further than Pisgah. But he believed. He believed in himself, in America, in man, in God, and in that faith he climbed the steps of the altar.

He was at once a poet and a prophet; he had that intuition which is the common differential of both — that insight which is foresight. For hear him, when leaving Springfield for "a duty greater than has devolved upon any man since Washington"—"unless the great God who assisted him shall be with me and aid me, I must fail: but if the same omniscient and almighty arm that directed and protected him shall guide and support me, I shall not fail—I shall succeed." By that token so was it unto him. I read and reread that pathetic invocation, I trace his growing trust in supreme mercy, I witness him "lead the whole nation thro paths of repentance and submission to the Divine will," I hear him urge "humble penitence for national perverseness and disobedience," and as our representative and spokesman say, "If every drop of blood drawn by the lash thro years of unrequited toil shall be repaid by one drawn by the bullet, still must we say our God is righteous." I see him not shrinking nor counting the chances of his own life. And blessing God for such a heart-born testimony as that one more, — "Die when I may, I want it said of me by those who knew me best that I always plucked a thistle and planted a flower where I thought a flower would grow,"— I challenge those who question his intrinsic truth toward the Highest.

Whatever were his speculative doubts, born of wholly inadequate religious teaching and hetchelled by experiences that embitter many—justice, mercy, humility, reverence, love, steadfast submission to God's will and way, these are the elements of the piety that Heaven accepts. He learned to pray and to intercede, and thro a temperate life he pitied the widow and the fatherless and kept himself unspotted from the world. "Pure religion and undefiled before God and the Father is this." Who loves what Christ loves, loves Christ. This high faith availed him in all affairs. He was no vagarist. Yet seeing and seizing the possible, he strove toward the stars. He was the most practical of idealists, believing that what should be can be, and that what should be and can be, shall be!

*Per aspera ad astra*—thro stripes to stars, for that stands our dear flag. It is the seal of the national wedlock, between each state and the Union, and that which God hath joined together no man shall put asunder!

"Hard, heavy, knotty, gnarly, backed with wrath," says Herndon, were Lincoln's words as in '56 he joined the party pledged to resist the extension of slavery.

Lincoln felt the unconscious destiny of America and helped, in the forefront, to abate the taunt of the world that our eagle was but a vulture. In that stumbling and disastrous night his soul was one that believed in the morning. Only a base and bastard mind can forget that he was part of the great price wherewith we obtained this freedom. The lost cause of caste was a triumphant failure. It freed the white man most.

> " We ignorant of ourselves,
> Beg often our own harms, which the wise powers
> Deny us for our good. So find we profit
> By losing of our prayers."

"The struggle of today (said Lincoln's message of December, 1861) is for a vast future also." Thankfully I quote from a true poet:

> "I love the South. I fought for her
>   From Lookout Mountain to the sea,
> But from my lips thanksgivings broke,
>   When that black idol, breeding drouth
>   And dearth of human sympathy
>   Thro all our sweet and sensuous South,
> Was, with its chains and human yoke,
>   Blown hell-ward from the cannon's mouth,
> While Freedom cheered behind the smoke."

Gentlemen, recall, you who can, that Good Friday — all those April days — of 1865, when God "shewed us hard things and made us to drink of the wine of astonishment," when all our victory was turned into mourning!

First, horror, then incredulity, then anguish — one wild, convulsed sob, "It can not, must not, shall not, be!" And then the reeling certainty that it was, and an orphaned nation calling, "My father, my father, the chariot of Israel and the horsemen thereof!" All the lowly of the Earth mourned, and in that mourning took hope for the universal cause of the people, and so the great conclave of universal hearts canonized him by acclaim. Party passions withered in that august homage. Factious critics and envious detractors stood abashed or repentant. In the knowledge of what it had lost the land first realized what it had had. So that catafalque moved thro its slow procession of twelve hundred miles. Dirges, minute guns, flambeaus, choirs, bells, and everywhere black misery and piteous tears — at last, Springfield. The faithful tomb unveiled its bosom to take to its trust this new treasure, and the troubled soul was at peace. But already that soul had begun to keep its endless Easter. The hand that penned the proclamation has touched the hand of that lost child whom the father's heart had never ceased to mourn. Those steps have come out of tribulation and found that One who "saved others and himself could not save." An offering? Yes — his own tired and thankful soul! A gift? Yes — not a scepter, but a pen; not a crown, but a broken manacle. "Well done, good and"—the gates are closed!

Once more I cite Abraham Lincoln: "We cannot escape history. The fiery trial thro which we pass will light us down in honor or dishonor to the latest generation"—to honor, noble one! Contrasted with the achievements of mere conquerors, how poor is all their prowess and ambition. Where is Bonaparte by the side of that tall spirit. Lincoln has one solitary peer in history—William of Orange, like himself, a martyr to his patriotism. The first administration of Washington gives parallel in the state of the army, the treasury and public opinion: but these were not war. The sorrow for Hamilton is an analogue. I think of these three as the three greatest Americans.

If Lincoln had not the charm of Hamilton and the urbane dignity of Washington, he had a sagacity rivaling the one, a patience rivaling the other, and a tenacity that surpassed them both. But I would not compare them; I would blend them all. They have passed under Time's impartial and dispassionate recognition. The place of Lincoln is secure in the judgment of mankind. Words can add nothing now to that monolithic fame. Death hath no more dominion over him. He was the pre-eminent man of the century that is hurrying to its end. Let the ascription of the French people, so significant in its allusion to the lower empire, stand as our last tribute—"He saved the Republic without veiling the statue of Liberty."

# Our Puritan Forbears

## ADDRESS BEFORE THE NEW ENGLAND SOCIETY AT ITS EIGHTY-EIGHTH ANNIVERSARY

### DECEMBER 22, 1893

*Mr. President, and Fellow-men* — The honors of this opportunity, as I well know, are not my own, but belong to my college mother.  That college, to which you owe your new President, tonight to be inducted; to whom Hartford owes those two great citizens, Senator Hawley and that delightful speaker whom presently we are to hear, and whose "journeys in the world" have never weaned him from his Alma Mater. [Applause.]

We bear the name and studiously expound the fame of that Scottish Huguenot than whom this imperial State never claimed a nobler or more potent son.  Patriot, jurist, financier, orator, statesman, father of the Constitution, Alexander Hamilton [strong applause], *clarum et venerabile nomen* — who of this company, in the city where his dust waits the last reveille, will not gladly acknowledge the legacy of that great Federalist, who said: "If they break this Union they will break my heart!" To us he is dear as the counsellor of our beginnings — our generous first almoner, our earliest trustee. [Applause.]

I come from a village named for that Scotch-Irishman who so long governed this Commonwealth, George Clinton, and from the glint of the stream which a little to the north witnessed that bloody afternoon of the Oriskany fight, where with shattered knee Herkimer sat smoking his pipe and issuing orders, while the German colonists of the valley blocked St. Leger and saved Stanwix and the Mohawk and the Hudson and New England and the cause. [Prolonged applause.] We who were born in her lap will not let you forget your debt to the pioneers of Oneida County.

Right on the earliest slope of our college hill a stone becarved with totems notes the secant of the "line of property" which by Johnson's treaty of 1768 set a "thus far only" to the East and bounded the perpetual West.

In the earlier days their loving missionary, and thereby strong with the Oneidas in those good diplomacies which in their critical value made Washington and Hamilton and Steuben his friends — Samuel Kirkland, son of Connecticut, came thither again in 1793 to be the founder whom we venerate, and the spirit of whose prayer to "the God of Wisdom" we would ever maintain. There he wrought and there he sleeps.

Where gentlemen, can we turn and not find common ancestors who were strong, true and prophetic? The best of our heritage is our lineage. Only supine ignorance and recreant neglect can alienate it. No anodyne, but a tonic — the story of those sturdy, believing, irreparable men — should tutor our courage while it shames our vanity. [Applause.]

One has shrewdly said: "When a man's talk is mainly of his ancestors, you may know that the best of the family is underground." [Laughter.] That is keen, but it is not true when retrospect teaches humility and stirs emulation. To come here to "garnish the sepulchres of our prophets" may be a sorry self-accusation, or it may be a regenerate pledge to those immortal and ever ennobling issues which their fidelities defined. [Applause.] Let that be true of us each which our Yankee Montaigne said of Landor: "He has examined before he has expatiated." If all the tale has long since been copyrighted, we may at least make repetition original by the accent of a new purpose, by an emphasis that — life, fortune, honor — shall add to our forbears — ourselves. No torso of rhetoric shall be such a tribute as the whole resemblance of a manhood that utters an intelligent *noblesse oblige*.

He was a sapient fellow who thought it "so fortunate that all the great cities had great rivers to run by them:" but when we merely flatter our Fathers for having ourselves as children we make the same ludicrous inversion of cause and effect. [Laughter and applause.] They are no discovery or invention of ours. They are the rivers, and well may we build by them.

Not about any slender and scantling facts has your society gathered all these years, and these facts are accessible and heroic. Levity ill becomes their gravity. I for one would as soon attempt a parody of the Dies Irae as to make mirth of that manly price which obtained the freedom into which we were born.

A certain sea captain wrote in his log: "The first mate drunk all day." "But," protested that officer, "it was but once for a year, and your record implies that I am a common sot." "Is it true?" asked the captain. "Then let it stand." The mate's turn came to write the log and he set down: "The captain has been sober all day." "What do you mean, sir?" roared the irate shipmaster. "Is it not true!" was the reply. [Laughter.]

We can distort facts by isolating them. We may caricature the Puritan by diverting to the wart of his foibles that heed which we owe to his full-length virtues. It promotes fun and also falsehood. The way in which some cross-eyed critics of these men, who so largely wore their ears snipped, "damn the sins *they* have no mind to," the sins of austere conviction and of obstinate righteousness, reminds me, in a way, of an authentic story of Pius IX. *Il Papa* was a wit and a smoker. One day in his private apartments, offering cigars to a group of ecclesiastics, one declined with, "No, Your Holiness, I have not that vice." While the rest looked aghast, the Pope with twinkling speed replied, "Ah, my good Bishop, if it were a vice you would have it." [Laughter.]

There is a temper toward our progenitors which, affecting self-complacency, comes close to the perilous edge of hypocrisy, for cant may also wear silk and dine sumptuously. Of the Puritan life, conquering and to conquer, that may be said which, of the same cause, Beza affirmed to the Queen of Navarre: "May it please Your Majesty to remember, the

Church of God is an anvil that has worn out many hammers."
Our forefathers! Where shall we begin and where end?
Seven generations back, and they become sixty-four fathers,
(you can do it upon your fingers.) A little further back, and
there is no end of them. Please God, there shall be no end.
They are "after the order of Melchisedec." But who shall be
your Atlas to stand up under this great epic?

Alas! I fear to be as that Methodist minister who ended his
sermon: "Brethren, I have had a great subject, but it has
caved in on me." [Laughter.]

First, in London, and about 1564, the "Puritans" received
the nickname that was to become a talisman. But that for
which the name stood, of pureness of public law, of religious
ceremonial, of private life, was wider than any Tudor domain.
It was international. In the name of the rights of God and of
the rights of man, it clamored with divers tongues, and in
many lands.

Our forefathers! They were Huguenot, Irish, Scotch, Welsh,
and withal they had the sinews of the men of Haarlem and
Leyden, of that people who, in both the data and the details of
human liberty, were, in 1600, a century in the van; that people
who educated for the British throne the logical and moral heir
of Cromwell, William III., so far as the miscellaneous line of
English royalty goes, a man with few predecessors and no
heirs.

But if our fathers—polyglot becoming Pentecost—were all
these, they were more—they were themselves. They had descent and precedent; they had also originality. Some things
they imported, some things were home-made here. But fully
and thankfully owning the composite metal which God has
brought out of the crucible, let us take that type of the Puritan
which we know best.

Those English apostles of all liberty did not go out from the
Church as by fiat established. They were thrust out. And yet,
deprived, defamed, proscribed, they were the stanchest upholders of the Crown. It took them sixty bitter years to learn how

brittle is a royal oath and to put no confidence in princes. What that selfish Queen would have made them they could not endure, but with their counsel and their courage they were the surest buttresses of her menaced throne. John Stubbs, printer, was one of them. He had written against the calculating flirtation with that saintly demon, Philip III., and for his offensive plainness was condemned to lose his hand. He wrote a plea as chivalrous as any that Sidney could have penned, that sentence might be revoked: but Elizabeth Tudor never knew pity, and he suffered. Leaping up from that mutilation, John Stubbs waved above his head the stump, spouting blood, and cried, "God Save the Queen! God save the—" and so fainted. That was Puritanism then.

Time wrought. From brave Peter Wentworth in the Commons, in 1572, down thro Eliot and Hampden and Pym, the voice sounded out and on for higher law than prerogative, ever deeper, fuller, more resolute. These men knew bonds and mutilations and the loss of all things. They crowded Bridewell, Newgate and the Fleet. They languished unjudged. They dwelt upon intimate terms with death. They were harried by sceptre and crosier. Bancroft and Whitgift lorded it over God's heritage, but their victims were constant. That bad triumvirate, Finch, Strafford and Laud, tormented them, but the cause grew and multiplied.

Came James I., of odious meanness, of adroit duplicity, of unspeakable profligacy. Came Charles I., that master of indecision—model of stubborn irresolution—that James Buchanan of the seventeenth century. [Laughter and applause.] Charles, called the martyr, supple in equivocation, a liar by wholesale and retail, with a royal disregard of oaths, and a regal incapacity for apprehending that the world was moving. Perfidy, sycophancy, usurpation went on; Star Chamber and Court of High Commission, differing in name only from Inquisition, were blind to the writing on the walls. . And Cromwell came, the soul and fist of political puritanism, of whom Taine says: "He was a man struck by the idea of duty." A man after the thing itself,—real, curt, masterful, direct. With wide, deep eyes, he saw those ideals for which England was yet unripe. He could not give England what she could not receive. He passed. They spiked his terrible head at Tyburn Bar. The cause of the people had no other human Protector. It seemed lost. But it was not lost; for the permanent results of the Commonwealth, which Guizot sums up in these words—"The downfall of absolute monarchy, the assured preponderance of the Commons, and the permanence of religious freedom"—these lasted as the tripod of English liberties. Under the compost heap of the Restoration lay the sure seed. It was Cromwell who, under God, was to find his true successors in Cobden, Bright and Gladstone. [Applause.] Shame to any Englishman who renounces the name of that great emancipator— Oliver, the first and the last.

But John the Baptist was gone, and the Herods were back. The populace reverted to "the leeks, the garlics and the cucumbers," and Whitehall again reeked with gay orgies. All things seemed to relapse. Stratagem, corruption and pusillanimous subservience to France rose to a flood that not even the genius of Clarendon could stem. The bishops, as the creatures of royalty, and sometimes the appointees of courtesans, turned on their stomachs as on a pivot. Adulation revamped its blasphemies. Then Charles II. went to rot with his memory, and the Duke of York reigned in his stead. But at length England, by very nausea, had learned the impossibility of the Stuarts, and would have no more of the varlet race. At last the Petition of Rights had come before that court "where sits a Judge no king can corrupt." Puritanism had wrought well. There had been excesses, vagaries, absurdities, partly *post hoc*, and partly *propter hoc;* but I, for one, appeal from the pen of Samuel Butler to the pen of John Milton, from the "Book of Sports" to the Word of God, and recall the testimony of Hume, himself a Tory,—"It is to the Puritan alone that England owes the whole freedom of her Constitution."

The cause of equal rights, the doctrine of "liberty and zeal," found its avatar in the Ironsides. Up from Lincoln and Norfolk and Essex and Kent swarmed the men whose sires Wyckliffe had emancipated, and who had stood to their pikes in the Low Country against the myrmidons of Alva. They were not humorists; life had been to them too stern and strenuous: but they had been schooled in the terse directness of the English Bible, and uplifted by its motive, its appeal, its boundless scope. They did not lack imagination nor hope. Easily they adopted the figures and terms of that "people's book." They, too, were fronting Philistia and Babylon. They made their own the war-words of Joshua and Jehoshaphat, and the exultant pæans of Miriam and Deborah. They gripped their stout tools at Naseby and at Preston with the challenges, "Quit you, like men," "Bind their kings with chains, and their nobles with fetters of iron," and between the hills and the sea they set their high psalm, "Arise, O God, and let thine enemies be scattered," and wrenched the victory at Dunbar. [Applause.]

Well did Curtis, whose silver bugle is now, alas! silenced, say of them: "If they snuffled in prayer, they smote in the fight; if they sang thro their noses, the hymn they chanted was Liberty."

May 29, 1660, the Parliament army was drawn up on Blackheath to receive Charles II., and then disbanded. They would march no more! No more? Nay—evermore! That spirit could not be mustered out. They rally again. It is to stand fire on Lexington Green; to "fire for God's sake" at Concord; shirt-sleeved and bare-headed to man the stone walls of the Boston Road; snatching their flint-locks by the barrel, to win that victory in defeat at Charlestown! "I cannot understand," said an Englishman, "why you make such a fuss over that monument. Who won that fight?" "Who kept the hill?" answered the American. It was the blood of Marston Moor that sent the husband of Mollie Stark from Londonderry to

Bennington, and that, by the command of that Connecticut Vermonter, bade Ticonderoga surrender "in the name of Jehovah and the Continental Congress." It was that spirit which yet makes all Connecticut men the children of Israel Putnam. It was Cromwellian determination that breathed again in Sam Adams, and Cromwellian valor, smiting home at Trenton and Monmouth, and enduring at Valley Forge, that at last took the sword of my Lord Cornwallis at Yorktown.

Disbanded? Nay! "Fall in! fall in, Ironsides!" thundered the guns of Robert Anderson, and down thro Baltimore trooped the men of Lynn and Marblehead. The theories of Roundhead and Cavalier grappled once again to make the ground of Virginia classic forever, and holy as the stairs of an altar. We can all of us, at this remove from that second and sterner clench, speak reverently of the nobility of Robert Lee and 'Stonewall' Jackson, and blend their names with our dearest heroes. What their personal nobility failed to do, surely no weaker arm can dare attempt. Their swords, too, are American.

Wherever the New England spirit had gone, thence her children's sons went down to the clench of Gettysburg and Chickamauga, to Hampton Roads and Mobile, until century replied to century, and Worcester's fight was sequelled at Appomattox. [Prolonged applause.]

If the day demands, the State of Nathan Hale [applause] can furnish other Ossawatomie Browns [thunders of applause] to lead the forlorn hope of those whose cries have come into the ears of the God of Sabaoth, and other Whittiers can set to their lips the terrible trumps of judgment.

Never until duty, "stern daughter of the voice of God," shall cease to speak, can the work of the Ironsides be ended.

We know the story of Scrooby and Amsterdam and Leyden and Delft Haven, of Brewster and Carver and Standish and Bradford, of dear Pastor Robinson, who testified of the breaking light, and said: "It is not with us as with men whom small things can discourage." [Applause.]

We know that boat (no bigger) of one-hundred-and-eighty tons, of the one-hundred-and-one souls who shipped in her, the torment of the seas, the bleak December, the new Ararat within the curved arm with which Massachusetts shakes her fist at all the world, the struggle to exist, the Colony five times decimated, the tedious and bare years. Yes, and we know renegade Peters and his fabrications. Knowing all about the Quakers and Roger Williams and Ann Hutchinson, we now claim them, too, as ours and Time's.

We recall the horrible delusion that found its twenty hapless victims, and see how those fathers fell below their ideals, as what greatness does not? But we recall also that Matthew Hale burned witches in England, and we do not forget the bitter persecutions of Presbyterians in Virginia and on this island down to 1775.

Withal, we see the marvelous power of true Puritanism to learn to confess its sins, to amend itself, to outgrow errors, its hospitality to new light, its genius for self-rectification. This great impulse has done what it was led hither that it might do—it has outgrown mediæval England. [Applause.] Its infallibilities are not of the past, but of things hoped for.

They were men of like passions with ourselves. We do not worship them; but we revere them. We do not organize a cultus; we accept an inspiration. They loved their land and their language. The white hills of Devon were in their hearts, as they named their Plymouth after the last they saw of Old England; but they "desired a better country." And so, holding the fireside sacred, and calling their babes after the heroes of the Old Testament and the virtues of the New, they wedded and wept and warred and worshipped, and ever they wrought, "by the armor of righteousness, by evil report and good report, as chastened and not killed; as sorrowful, yet always rejoicing; as poor, yet making many rich; as having nothing, and yet possessing all things." They "feared not the wrath of kings," for the shout of that other King was among them; and so of them also it was true, "a nation and a company of nations shall be of thee, and kings shall come out of thy loins." With sublime unconsciousness, they were shaping institutions of which they never dreamed, but always tenaciously affirming the ideals which are the base of these institutions, and without which we can neither understand nor maintain them. [Applause.]

The best of them were what the best of you would then have been, and the best of you are what the best of them would now be.

They magnified those influences without which great things could no more be fulfilled than Dakota could ripen her wheat by moonlight. They trusted the chemistry of noonday truth. They revered and they practised that law which alone, of all the codes of time, ordains for labor fifty-two holidays in every year, and they proved that God will bless the land where every week is bounded on the west by rest and prayer. These heirs of Latimer, Knox, Coligny, Prince Maurice knew why they had moved so far. They had a religion that bore transplanting. They nursed those "household virtues whereon rests the unconquerable state," and sung the cradle songs that are the true foundation of anthems. We cannot take out of our bone and fibre the stuff our forefathers have put there. If it is so much more comfortable to be a Buddhist in Boston than in Bombay, it is Puritanism that has made it so: but we cannot long renounce the high obligation and retain the wide benefit; for that which made this a land worth coming to will alone keep it a land worth staying in! [Applause.]

The prevailing forces of this, our country, have been Saxon and Norse and Teutonic, not Latin.

We are not French, *La gloire* is not American glory, and *l'amour* is not American love. We are not Spanish. We will not be Italian. I love the Italy of Dante, of Bruno and Savonarola, of Galileo and Garibaldi; but not the Italy of those who stifled or rejected these. [Applause.]

Let our Washington still be heard: "Resist with care the spirit of innovation, however specious the pretexts. . . . Against the insidious wiles of foreign influence (I conjure you to believe me, fellow-citizens) the jealousy of a free people ought to be constantly awake." [Tremendous cheering.]

Yes, great leader, we do believe; we will remember; God helping us, we will not become the acolytes of a system our fathers suffered so to renounce. The Potomac shall not become an affluent of the Tiber. We need no larger infusion of priestcraft into politics. Let all super-serviceable Satollis, and satellites whatsoever, learn that the American eagle is not that kind of a bird! We stand by the old watchwords—a free State, free churches, a free press and free schools. [Prolonged applause.] One hundred years our ancestors wore the nickname, but the thing they achieved shall, God grant, be the empire of a thousand years.

When was there ever a fitter time than now to bring into affairs the stern conscience of the Fathers? Where a more suitable place for it than Manhattan Island? Think how you will need it when you are no longer compelled to swim your Hellespont to fondle New Jersey! And think, too, in behalf of New Jersey! You may build your Washington arches and your Grant tombs, you may fill your parks with eloquent bronze; but what a loftier tribute would it be to these memories—to the memory of such as Hamilton and Jay—to make the municipal rule of New York City respectable! What men are more divinely called than those I speak to, to forswear the dastardliness of indifferentism, to see that of all "dangerous classes" the sybarites and shirks are the worst, to remember that *tacet* soon becomes *licet*, that to permit rascals is to promote them and be their quiet accomplices?

Straining hopes look to us. The peoples of Europe—"not thrones and crowns, but men," whose leaders, staggering to the brink of bankruptcy, yet stare with fierce, unforgiving eyes over ever-widening lines of scientific iron—piteously appeal to us to be true to our trust!

Talismanic land! As America goes, so goes the world; but as the cities go, so goes America! Let us not flinch from our tasks if we would be enrolled with our fathers.

Emerson said of Boston: "Her annals are inextricably national." It is true of all that region of "man-bearing granite."

New England, mother of constitutions, of States, of Senators, of churches, of missions, of colleges, of armies, of inventions, of ideas, of men! And I will drink the pledge in that element which was to our fathers at once a bridge and a bastion—in water, as clear as the bright dews of baptism, as pure as that which gurgled down the sands at Plymouth. [Prolonged and repeated applause.]

## The Duty of Enthusiasm

*AN ADDRESS DELIVERED AT THE CELEBRATION OF INDEPENDENCE DAY WOODSTOCK, CONN., JULY 4, 1894*

---

*Mr. President, Sisters and Brothers*—One may well pray to be delivered both from his traducers and his introducers! Having already suffered many things of many presidents, I am once more the victim of circumstances. Presently you each shall be! I have been delighted, as you have been, to hear the honorable member from the Worcester District sauce Massachusetts. [Laughter.] No one outside the bounds of Massachusetts dare speak his mind so freely about Harvard College. Perhaps I should begin the words I have to say with apology for ever having graduated from a college! And should make further apology for having anything to do with a college faculty. But I do not impugn the logic of my friend; for I remember that there are colleges and colleges, that, as "they didn't know everything down in Judee," so they do not know everything even in the great colleges of New England, tho they know a little of everything. There are colleges and colleges, there are Congressmen and Congressmen. Our friend does not want free sugar in his, but some Congressmen do. I desire, this morning, to put myself outside the range of his syllogisms, and to say that however humble may be my relation to college work I will not stand in the shoes of any cold-blooded expounder of what has been so well called 'the dismal science,' because, first it leaves out God, and second, it leaves out man. [Applause.]

"That's it," Mr. Walker? Thank you.

I say Amen to some things, not to everything that you have

stated. I am sound on this question. There has been some little discussion because the college with which I am connected, in Central New York, has lately declined the formal leading strings of the Presbyterian Synod of New York, and I told some friends who were questioning our ecclesiastical polity, if no more, that we were sufficiently sound on that matter, and to prove it to them I quoted a prayer that my little boy, eight years of age, made at his mother's knee, in which he said: "O Lord, help me not to branch off into any other religion. Help me always to be a good Presbyterian, and not a Mormon, or anything like that!" [Laughter.]

This is not my first and I hope it will not be my last chance to detain the ears of New Englanders. It is hard to hold on and dangerous to let go! There is a certain independence in speaking to those who are like the farmer to whom Whitter loaned his copy of Plato, and who came back saying: "I like that fellow; he has some of my ideas." [Laughter.] The New Englander takes his ideas always mixed with brains. The multitude of those who are gathered here today are not to be measured by arithmetic, but by ethics, rather. New Englanders are not to be counted, but are to be weighed. They come not by the dozen, but by the pound. Before this representative audience I feel as if I were speaking into a telephone that had universal connections. I hope that I shall be heard at the other end of the line with that emphasis which was illustrated at one of the earliest telephones, when a farmer went into the office and, having had the thing explained to him, was asked to put his ear to it. He called up his wife. Just then there came a clap of thunder. He exclaimed: "That's Maria!" He recognized the voice. [Laughter.] One of our speakers said something about the boycotts that were such a trouble, or blessing not unmixed, and a friend of mine, who always sits very near to me, suggested that the girl-cotts had something to do with it, too. [Laughter.] I am thankful for both the boycotts and the girl-cotts of that sort. I think the women, who make the majority of this and perhaps every other crowd in New England — and out of it, too — where brains are at all in demand, may well take comfort to themselves from a sentiment which was given at a New England dinner in New York, where one, proposing an impromptu toast to the Pilgrim Mothers, said, They endured all that the Pilgrim Fathers endured, and they endured the Pilgrim Fathers besides! [Laughter.]

I am glad we started off today with "Yankee Doodle." It is great, classic with something better than classicism. Every New Englander ought to know that story of how the first regiment went down from these hills that so ballast the memories of an honorable race. They were gathered into the Astor House in New York, the first New England regiment to go to the front. Broadway from curb to curb was thronged, and as the first glitter and flash of the front file issued from the doorway of that historic inn, about ten o'clock in the morning, the band struck up "Yankee Doodle," of all tunes in the world. The people set up such a mighty roar and tempest of sympathy and determination as seemed to rock the very granite walls. There was no uncertainty after New England had set that tune of how the city of New York would go! [Applause.]

We stand within the bounds of no mean commonwealth, rather of one whose historic honor is so bright that when one reads her annals it is to wonder what is left to record for the fame of the other stars of our constellation. It is a record legible and luminous all the way from Buckingham to Morris. Under what better motto could we gather than Connecticut's "*Qui transtulit sustinet*"! But today, men and women of a score of States, perhaps of every State, where that dear banner answers the heavens with its stellar and auroral beauty — today we are each and all Americans! [Applause.] Thanks to the host who calls us here! Joy to the hearts that answer him! Peace, plenty, above all piety, unsullied, unbounded, unfaltering, to the land we love and call our own! But we are all here not only to remember; we are also here to resolve, highly, humbly, fervently and with unanimous consecration. No one can attempt to voice your wills today with a deeper sense of inadequacy than mine is as I think how many notable and noble souls have brought their best to this illustrious rendezvous. How poor shall be the largest that the best can bring to this great love-feast of our loyalty!

Dear America! "Beautiful my country!" "Nation and company of nations!" I hail my privilege to lay my offering among the laurels of this day of days. Massachusetts, the mother of Adams; New York, proud foster mother of Alexander Hamilton; Illinois, dear to us forever for those two sons of Anak who smote home for the cause of mankind's emancipation and enfranchisement — I have loved all these with a filial love: but were any or all of them to lift recreant and insane hands against the District of Columbia, I am for my whole country! Thank God, undistinguishable, indisseverable, all those stars blend in one ever-crescent light. How shall Texas say "This is mine," or Ohio say "This is mine?" All are ours, and we are for them all! [Applause.]

But we are here for a mission. That were but tawdry declamation that should deal in glittering vagueness. A duty summons us — a divine, a holy trust is in our hands, at such an hour, in such a land, where still portent and promise so strangely blend. It is ours in the name of the fathers, to recognize the demands upon our total powers, and to pledge ourselves that the hastening future of our fatherland shall be epical and not tragic.

I am to speak to you of THE DUTY OF ENTHUSIASM. I wanted a big text, and there it is. *Enthusiasm* is a great word. A true master, who gave language new force by his idiomatic use of it — Isaac Taylor — once wrote a book upon the " Natural History of Enthusiasm." But his whole treatment of that theme dealt with the lower and oblique associations of the word, and warned against perverse, unreasoned and mistaken zeal. He noted the quixotic and fanatical elements of the mere rhapsodist — the dogmatism and violence of the self-opinionate — the passion that lacks wisdom, and the ecstacy that is sanguine without sense. It is of the better and truer significance of Enthusiasm that I would speak. The word means — full of the god. It shall stand with us for inspiration, for consecration, for that joyful and dauntless purpose which never rests in the superficiality of averages and which hastens the kingdom of that truth which it is persuaded of and hails from afar. True enthusiasm means daring and uncompromising devotion. It is not a sentiment and an intoxicant, but an ardent and quenchless hope that what should be shall be! This is dedication — the sublime surrender of the whole being to the guidance of the ever-on-going God. And this is duty. Because it is a duty it is a possibility. It is our privilege and our right. I summon your souls to see that nothing less than such a surrender to our Maker can answer the voices of the times and fulfill the obligations of high manhood and womanhood. [Applause.]

It is the conquest of the soul by great and profound ideas that makes great. This is the stuff whereof pioneers and prophets are made. Said Swedenborg: "Such as the love is, such is the wisdom." Men see with their hearts, and the heart that counts no sacrifice costly if ultimate truth may reign, is the heart that is 'full of the god'. The three great elements of power are these — judgment, imagination, hope. He who has these is complete and furnished to every good work. One may have either without the others — then he is gibbous instead of spherical. The true leader and the true follower — each is one who will take great risks for great reasons.

> " He either fears his fate too much,
>   Or his deserts are small,
> Who will not put it to the touch,
>   And win or lose it all."

## IMPLACABLE MANHOOD

But this non-prudential eagerness does not forget the critical, it rather consummates its conclusions in executive decisions. There is today a cant of moderation. It is one of the affectations of conventional propriety to suppress impulse and to cry down intensity of conviction. This *blasé* theory of behavior, this *ennui* of life, avoids elemental seriousness. It never breathes deep enough to breathe hard. It skims the mere rim of reality. It dwells in petty fads, and gushes over them with abundant adjectives. It is superlative because it is not positive, and takes the whole English language in vain to ornament a whim. It lives in the subjunctive instead of the indicative mood. It wishes, but it never wills. The simulation of enthusiasm is its death. Shallow intent destroys the very capacity of high thoughts and deep life. Dawdling selfishness is the damnation of dudes and impotents.

> "For life is not as idle ore,
>   But iron dug from central gloom,
> And heated hot with burning fears,
> And dipped in baths of hissing tears,
>   And battered with the stroke of doom,
> To shape and use."

We need to get by heart Paul's characterization of Epaphroditus, who "for the work of God was nigh unto death, staking his life."

A wise Frenchman wrote a book under the proposition that "Eloquence is a Virtue." It is a faithful saying. When the real man arrives he speaks with tones that smite his time of stupidity as the thunders break the oppression of the heavy summer day. John the Baptist, Martin Luther, Cromwell, Mirabeau, Sam. Adams, O'Connell, John Bright, Garrison, Phillips, Lincoln — these are the men whose enthusiasm interrupts and crushes the stolidity of custom and the irresolution of policy. The great orator is the implacable *man*. With molten speech, with the naked power of a conviction that scorns half-truths, a terror to the bad and to the timid, impeaching that absolute infidelity to the hour and to the opportunity which often intrenches itself in the most consummate orthodoxy *in thesi*—not sinister and never merely dextrous, but two-handed and whole-hearted the Voice leaps alive into the midst of a stagnant and querulous time, challenging its practical atheisms with all the sublimity and mastery of the truth itself. Such men God sends as the couriers of repentance, and they are the herald-angels of the Evangel. They disdain the paltry evasions and subterfuges of expediency, and trembling themselves in the reality of that kindling ideal which both consumes and compels them—taking fire like meteors by the rapidity and friction of their passage—they are the avatars of the message they announce! [Applause.]

But to us all God is ever saying: "Whom shall we send, and who will go for us?" A deep voice sounding out the lonely truth is like a midnight bell; it rings into innumerable ears, which wake and listen and thank God for another day. God guide and guard that prophet who, in the face of vast reproach, is rousing the hypnotized conscience of Manhattan Island. [Applause.] The Tammany Goliath may vaunt, and the Republican Eliab may sneer, but this last David, not in the Saul's armor of the place-holder and pelf-distributor, but with the smooth stone slung true shall slay his tens of thousands. The one great mission of the Hebrew Prophets was to preach righteousness *to their times*—they were in politics for all they were worth! It is an antedeluvian heresy that denies the right or neglects the duty of such an enthusiasm as knows how to perceive the power of contemporary iniquity and to arraign it with the voice of a Micaiah or a Joel. [Applause.]

Enthusiasm is the characteristic alike of the scientist, the historian, the poet, the true statesman, the apostle, the saint. Inspiration is the note and accent of every life that touches its age with the dateless law of duty. They who "prefer bondage with ease to strenuous liberty" are those who have said of the idols of material success—"these be thy gods." Shall it be Aaron, with the cultus of the calf—the worship of the visible

— or Moses, with "Thou shalt have no other God before me!" There is no slavery so blind as the prostitution of enthusiasm at the altars of Mammon — where today "the great man boweth down, and the mean man humbleth himself." The last question is, "Who shall reign?" The sovereignty of God is the final truth. Deep and ominous if we heed it not, the long roll is already beating, and from gate to gate the whisper will swell to a voice like the storm, "Who is on the Lord's side?"

Americans are, of all people on earth, most avid of congratulation and averse from censure. But a merely provincial patriotism that worships either knowledge, or skill, or strength, or plenty, will no more preserve our semi-Christian civilization from becoming godless than these saved Babylon! Americans do not love their Jeremiahs: but they well may heed them. We are not in such danger today from foreigners as we are from ourselves. I for one, because I am a patriot, will remember that the best part of the word "fatherland" is the first part; and, repudiating that toast of Stephen Decatur's, "Our Country, Right or Wrong," I will pray, "Our Father which art in Heaven," and, "Our Country Right, and Never Otherwise." *Vox Dei, vox populi*" must be the new patriotism. [Applause.] It is only the discipline of obedience to the high God that can apply the power of enthusiasm to public life. Eagerness of conscience must be trained, by common consent, to effective programs. We need today a new oath of allegiance to that God whom on our coinage we say we trust. We need to publish a new Declaration of *De*pendence. Public opinion is not infallible. Majorities are not final. Righteous minorities are the real rulers — not screaming themselves hoarse with that terrestrial apotheosis of man in the *"Aux armes les braves"* of the Marseillaise, but chorusing the deeper purpose and the sublimer enthusiasm of *"Ein feste Burg ist unser Gott!"* [Applause.]

Liberty's statue yonder in New York Harbor is but a hollow idol unless it upholds the lamp which God alone can kindle and keep! Providential America, daughter of privilege and opportunity, understand thyself by that philosophy of history which thine open Bible gives thee, by that enthusiasm, that fullness of God, whose prayers become prophecies!

> "For here is truest taught and easiest learnt
> What makes a nation happy and keeps it so,
> What ruins kingdoms and lays cities flat."

Upon the Saxon race lies the triune mission of Greek, Roman and Hebrew. It stands triply for culture, for law, for reverence. Not alone in these tongues, but in our own dear English let it be written—in the tongue of Wyckliffe and Milton, and Tennyson, and Whittier, and Lanier, "THIS IS THE KING"!

The Saxon never wore the yoke easily nor long. With the power of conscience and the enthusiasm of truth, he has conquered his conquerors. He may perish, but he can only perish by his own moral suicide. The Saxon is invited to the headship of the nations. He rules as Cæsar never dreamed of ruling. He holds the commanding influence in four continents, and is sole master of the fifth. He girdles the round Earth, with nations. His righteous will may be law for the planet. He must not swerve from God. Christ has raised up this solid front of a hundred million men. What pencil dipped in the dawn can write its possible glories, or dipped in the smoke of Hell can limn its obloquy! The switch points are set close for either line.

> "*Today* we fashion destiny, the web of fate we spin,
> *Today* for all hereafter choose we holiness or sin;
> 'E'en now from starry Gerizim or Ebal's cloudy crown
> We call the dews of blessing or the bolts of cursing down."

There is an optimism which boasts in its own strength, and there is a pessimism which cravenly invites the woes it dreads. There is a *tertium quid*, the cross of Christ; above us Heaven, beneath us the pit, about us God! Not optimism, not pessimism, but enthusiasm. There are dangers dire and dark, demagogs and monopolists, poltroons and panderers, with sophisms that slander manhood and doubts that slander God: but by the arm of God we can beat them down!

Back in 1871, when men in Chicago were hanging themselves to lamp-posts and drowning themselves in the lake, a man put an advertisement in one of the papers, reading: "Men of Chicago, take hope. Our fathers raised her from the bog, and we can raise her from the ashes!" It is that spirit that raised that Phenix City by the shore of Lake Michigan. It is in that Chica*go* spirit, translated and transfigured by the Gospel of Christ, that we need today, every one of us, to put whole souls into all affairs. [Applause.] God will give us light if we ask Him for it. Hope is creative, doubt is abortive. Let us hope, then act. The men who are willing to deny themselves any possible gain, who forget that a vote is a vow, who forget that a candidate is a man clad-in-white, who forget the patriotism of paying taxes, who forget that law is like a bicycle and that the way to keep it standing is to keep it going, whose very bones are flabby with civil neglect, whose minds are mere kennels for vagrant theories, and who recant the old-fashioned law of duty and "the faith that comes by self-control," (and by self-sacrifice, too,) these moral spendthrifts and soul paupers, these are the *incubi* of the times! Such a man is not a man, but a manikin. [Applause.] But upon the souls who are full of the enthusiasm of duty rests the unconquerable State. To these "the Christ that is to be" flings wide His effectual doors. Ruled by such a ken life can never seem shabby nor hope irrational. To him who truly lives and does, the veil of the visible becomes more and more diaphanous. There are such men. We do not always listen to hear the deep breathing of the people ready to respond to the prophet of conscience. We bite into one blasted ear, and forget the green sabers of the corn that array a thousand prairies. We find one brackish pool, and forget the trickling of a myriad translucent springs. We see one whirling, copper cloud, and doubt the Sun. But God reigns! God reigns!

On some level shores the tides rise, invisibly percolating all the sands.  One instant it is shore, and the next up comes the ocean and it is sea.  The ebb is no more, the flood tide is on. Such is the spontaneity and instantaneousness of many a great and invisibly gradual movement under the Sovereign Spirit.

Thou who didst steer the little "Mayflower" to her desired haven, bring America to port!  Grant that upon this gathering of the people our dear flag may shine with the light of an Evangel, pure as the sweet influences of the Pleiades and firm as the bands of Orion.  Thou who dost guide Arcturus, grant that those stars may glow in the coronet of Christ.  In the enthusiasm of loyalty to God, and serried against the evils and forebodings of the time, we will march in the footsteps of a believing ancestry.  Let every flagstaff and belfry, every throbbing dome and thundering cannon, every eloquent orator and voice of multitudes, every prayer of gratitude and every sob of joy, carry the name that is above every name, and swear it with a mighty oath: "This God is our God, as He was our father's God, and He shall be ours forever and forever."  So can we say, with all high confidence, after the great laureate now asleep:

> "Are there thunders moaning in the distance?
> Are there specters moving in the darkness?
> Trust the hand of light will guide His people
> Till the thunders pass, the specters vanish,
> Aud the light is victor, and the darkness
> Dawns into the jubilee of the ages."

**GOD SAVE AMERICA!**

# The Future of the Independent College

*AN ADDRESS GIVEN AT THE CONVENTION OF THE ASSOCIATION OF THE COLLEGES AND PREPARATORY SCHOOLS IN THE MIDDLE STATES AND MARYLAND AT THE JOHNS HOPKINS UNIVERSITY AT BALTIMORE DECEMBER 1, 1894*

*Ladies and Gentlemen*—The invitation given me to speak here was cheerfully accepted because of the introduction it assured to those from whom I am glad to learn. HAMILTON takes its place this year as a permanent unit in this Association. I find myself the fortunate successor to the good-will last year accorded to Professor Brandt, of our Faculty, who at that time represented us by a careful and critical paper. You may hereafter reckon upon us to take all proper share in the stimulating discussions which mark your annual sessions.

The question now before us has already been amply and adequately introduced, and with all deference to the gentlemen who have so surrounded the theme, I submit my remarks, quite aware that you will "piece out my imperfections with your thoughts."

The subject, as furnished me, was—"The Independent College as Distinguished from the University." Not as a doubter but as a believer, not as an outsider but as a loyal son of such a college, I venture to offer these paragraphs to your larger and elder experience. Endeavoring to deal with whatever is futuritive so as to find its relations to present fact and obvious tendency, I would avoid the role of either Balaam or Cassandra, and seek, tho least, a place among the canonical, if minor, prophets.

Until a recent period (epoch some of you might call it) the story of higher education in America has been the story of the 'Independent College.' By 'Independent,' I shall mean that which is not in absolute dependence upon a particular State or Church, which is self-governed and which is maintained by its own corporate enterprise.

The relation which any college sustains to the Christian church should be vital rather than formal, one of reciprocity but not of merged identity. Its status and responsibility should be moral rather than ecclesiastical, and in absolute freedom from the contingencies of denominational weather.

Prelatical or quasi-prelatical control is non-representative, and sacrifices philosophical breadth and progress to a special regime of polity.

Affinity and affiliation are far stronger and far freer and less inconstant than sectarian responsibility. They appeal to a larger constituency, in a nobler way, and with ampler assurances of both movement and stability. Moral relation is more than legal. It is not contradictory,—it is other and fuller, and it escapes both the caprice of casual majorities and the shadow of mortmain.

The denominational plea is too exclusive and too procrustean, and in so far as it is efficient it is narrowing. But the non-sectarian is not therefore the secular. Secularism is one of the most cramped of sects and its shibboleths are as arbitrary as any that can be imposed. Unhesitatingly I claim that substantive Christianity is both scientific and crescent. Only a polyglot and Babeled theory forgets the spatial horizon of that kingdom whose King of Truth offers the ultimate constructive standards of mental and moral life. These two are at last but one, and to magnify the mastery of second causes to the forgetting of origins and ends, is to rob thought of its profoundest realm, and to substitute a frustrum for the zenith.

The non-religious or contra-religious alleged learning, whose hopes are all horizontal and temporal, is neither beautiful nor rational. It deals with surds. What is genial (as Coleridge said of Shakesperean criticism) must be reverential. The world needs spherical not bulbous men. Its spiritual Philistinism can only be mastered by unshorn Samsons. Ethics of convention, of terrestrial expediencies, reveal their bastardy in their barrenness. The crossing of intellectual avidity with an undevout nescience is both hybrid and sterile, and against it the array of schools that have been maintained and blessed in the faith and fear of God must teach that a true biology leads on toward Him in whom all that lives has its being, that astronomy is the royal herald of the Light of the World — Πατὴρ τῶν φώτων —, that faith is the eye of scholarship, and that practical and expert manhood consists in bringing the loftiest motives to the lowliest tasks.

The latest word of science (writes Henry Drummond) is that "All nature is on the side of him who tries to rise." To that rising time sets no limits.

That College has an assured future which renounces all inferior dependence that it may be loyal to the Christian declaration of the rights and rule of the Highest. That College has an assured future which in history distinguishes between the dead who live and the living who are dead, and shows those whose gristle is soon to become bone, how modern mercantilism taints the moral sense, and how the idolatry of merely optical knowledge becomes sciolism.

Real education draws out the deepest faculties and bends them to their utmost functions.

"We live (says Principal Fairbairn) in the generation that has witnessed the transit of power, and this means that for the battle to maintain our place and fulfill our function in the history of humanity we have called out our last reserves! The earliest moments in the use of power must always be the most critical, for they are the formative moments. It is the people who now rule, and unless God live in and rule thro the people, the end of all our struggles, the goal of all our boasted progress will be chaos." The true school must scholar its product to serve the people—*the peoples*. The school, be its product more or less for quantity, must qualify that product to advantage mankind in the undermost necessities. Thus only can the school be saved from soulless dilletanteism and and minister to the profound and restless exigencies of the age.

(1) What I have so far said opens my first contention, namely, that *manhood* is the thing to be sought, evoked and equipped under the obligations of a celestial allegiance. I do not speak by way of disparagement; but affirming thus the standards of one "small College" whereof I know, I venture to assert that the three hundred smaller colleges of America are doing a work in instilling reverent and comprehensive motives which nothing else in America, on the whole, is like, and that neither the present nor the future can spare these labors nor their vast results. Their part is indeed coordinate with that of all special schools; but it is also peculiar, integral and indispensable.

(2) An important and peculiar mission of the College, as such, is its exponency and guardianship of all-around *discipline*, as discriminated from that special or technical training which the University, as such, must make its specific area and prime end. This matures and enlarges men for that.

The impulse of the representative *College* magnifies those ideals and enforces that patient drill which are the best of all preparation for thoroness in particular pursuits, be they scientific, literary, or professional. These widen the personal orbit, and confer both balance and momentum.

The significant and enduring literature of New England has thus far come from those who were lessoned and roused under the disciplines of a training strictly collegiate. It remains to be seen whether their successors shall on the whole excel them. The appliances and associations, the apparatus and the teachers who are using the old disciplinary methods, are now as in the past bent toward making pliant minds aware of their whole and best selves, and of their dutiful part toward what the ancients called "the wheel of life." I presume, however signal the pedagogic station of those who have uttered it, to controvert the proposition that "it is no longer worth while to uphold the idea of a liberal education."

The liberal arts — that is, in the old sense, those suitable for a freeman — still subtend the truest training of the man not servile. They temper and anneal. However useful or benign the after art, or exact the later science, either fares better with him who has been developed roundly by intelligent interest in many things. We cannot dispense with great investigators; but we must have a multitude of resolute and clear-visioned citizens to encourage and to appreciate these, and so to appropriate and extend their results. Physician or attorney, preacher or pedagog, jurist or juryman, the least near-sighted man will go the furthest. Early discipline is the best preventive of after pedantry. True education is a geometry of three dimensions. Narrow depth will be found as partial as shallow breadth. I plead for neither and against both. We want cubic men.

The discipline of a thoro-going undergraduate course prepares for the wisest and heartiest selection of the lifetime's work. Moreover it often does this by revealing aptitudes and rousing ambitions that else would have slept unguessed. It suggests and solicits choice. This discovery and motive service is acting upon latent talent thro all our land and finding what, acting alone, the University proper would never find.

I do not lack manifold assurances from experts in technical and professional schools that the soundest and best-grained material they get comes from the ranks of those who have not shunned the routines of a stiff general course in arts. I am so far constrained to think that the men who specialize least in College are the men who specialize best afterward. Could the Universities do their present work and forego the supply of this Bessemered man-material?

Rivalry and mutual disparagement can never well beseem

these complementary forces. The future can spare neither. They give the two foci of the education which is to be.

(3) And, yet again, quite apart from the vertical influences of the college training, I insist upon the lateral influences of *college association*. It consorts men. It is democratic. Its aristocracy is of the right sort. It reduces the tendency toward snobbery, even of the intellectual kind. Its romance is of essential value, fully realized, alas! by most of us, only when it is irreparably past, but containing a vital poetry we can never forget.

Those days of ideality and dreams! How the shreds of long-silenced songs sound on in the corridors of our hearts! That *microcosmos* — with zests, emulations, politics, achievements, all its own, swathed by an atmospheric force that rivals the curriculum as wings rival wheels! It is an intense epitome of the strenuous life to which it is the door. He who forgoes the eager, fervent, imaginative spirit of such a community of zeal and effort, misses what he may learn to regret but can never recover. That glamouring light shines only once.

The ruthless haste into affairs or professions which skips the ardors and aspirations of the "*collegisse juvat*" is self-robbery. I dare implead those who ignore this period of exceptional ideality, of generous sentiment, of manly, even if sometimes hasty, impulses, of hope, high and hot, of developing will that shall use after skill, of lifelong and unrivalled friendships.

Our college students with all their impetuous faults live a far deeper life than ever goes to print. This dormitory life with its keen criticism of common interests, its swift puncture of sham, its absolute appreciation of all that is fair, gallant and strong, makes many men better and makes few worse. American life, could ill spare the boisterous energies, the thrilling enthusiasms, the rousement and unsophisticated purpose of her college boys. For this, too, the College has a future. It cannot become an anachronism.

(4) Last I insist upon that direct relation, with its personal

knowledge and friendly interest, which the College favors and stimulates, and I cite the words of President Porter, words whose pertinency the recent interval of years has not diminished, and which are at once an eulogium and a confession. "A small college, (he wrote) well manned and thoroly administered, has many advantages over one that is larger in respect of the intimacy of acquaintance and intercourse between the officers and pupils, and also in respect of the vigor with which a few studies wisely selected can be thoroly enforced. The larger colleges have much to fear from the bulk and weight of the mass of material thrown upon their care, and from the growing tendency to exalt the professorial to the disadvantage of the tutorial function."

Truly; for beyond all instruction glows the sphere of inspiration. Information is much: but formation is more. The contagion of thoughtful and truth-devoted lives is subtile and swift. Our colleges, with keen regard to this result, must insist upon manning their every department with those who impersonate fineness and force and the "faith that comes by self-control."

Such they do seek and largely find; men who, because they themselves have enthusiasm, can both rouse and guide it, whose first specialty, with whatever else, is *influencing young men*. Sincere intercourse with high-minded and wide-minded teachers is the chief means to the best educational ends. Other things being even nearly equal the College where this is most realized is at the fore. This belongs characteristically to the College domain as it does not to the University, just as it is the captains rather than the colonels who know the rank and file of the regiments. The future cannot spare this constant element of leverage, and more and more, by every consideration, will the Colleges appreciate and use it.

And so, to approach the end, I submit that the term "small college" frequently puts a coarse-arithmetical appraisal in place of one that is dynamic and therein more just. In the comparison of ratios between their respective groups of effective and influential graduates, it is not always the little College that suffers. Colleges vary as the square of the ideals which they impart and vivify. Those are large that issue the largest *pro rata* of large men, and those are small whose man-product is relatively lesser in mental and executive efficiency. Those who are so ready to make a patronizing complaint that the College unduly attempts the functions of the University in advanced specialization should logically be as careful to see that the University should not usurp or minify the indispensable functions of the College.

Neither legitimately includes the other. The University has no more call to dictate the College course than the College has call to dictate the University course. The two are of right as distinct as they should be complemental.

The edges where they divide may and probably must slightly overlap, but this is no reason for friction, either by an airy and opulent condescension, or by a covetous and impatient ambition. There should be a self-respecting individuality in each task, and in the assertion and fulfilment of that individuality the utmost mutual regard and cooperation. Graduate or under-graduate course, let each affirm, honor and magnify its own peculiar and distinct occasion and sphere, ever more persistently, symmetrically, convincingly, and let neither envy and neither vaunt.

# Emma Willard

## AN ADDRESS AT THE PRESENTATION OF THE RUSSELL SAGE HALL IN TROY, N. Y. MAY 16, 1895

It is one of the high privileges of a college president to be put into relation with many noble enterprises and occasions that lie somewhat outside of his own strict sphere. It is also one of the penalties of such an office that its incumbent is often summoned to minister in matters that quite transcend his own special fitness.

But willingly I have met the cordial request of these twain whose united hearts and hands are responsible for this occasion, and most cheerfully I become the spokesman of an appreciation and gratitude which all now here share, and would, each, I am sure, desire to express and to augment. Most cordially I bring to this assembly, and, first of all, to these generous benefactors, the greetings of an institution that has a fraternal interest and zeal for whatever shall advance the cause of true and general education within the bounds of a state whose primacy in learning, in law, in civil and domestic character, in commercial enterprise and influence, in noble popular ideals and in all that promotes their realization, in reverent and religious purpose,—whose primacy in these things that make a commonwealth truly great, all the states of this august "family of nations" may well honor without envy and emulate without rivalling. The motto of this imperial New York of ours,—with its ardent six millions and its noble schools, colleges, churches and homes, its varied centres of manufacture and trade, its splendid thorofares of traffic and travel, its strong and earnest homogenity,—is a motto of perpetual ambition and betterment. EXCELSIOR is a device that was both a purpose and a prophecy. Vital labor is always the impulse and expression of hope. Manly hope, which must be hope for all that uplifts and unites *man*, can never tire nor pause in its outreach and upgoing. The New York of this generation is but an enlarging link between the New York that was and the New York that in God's providence is to be. To Him, under the word *Excelsior*, we are pledged, in the comparative degree,—pledged always to transcend present attainment in committing ourselves to more, larger, better things. We accept this onward step as a token of progress in this community and as a type of the duty to which all our Empire State is elected and divinely urged.

Zeal for the simultaneous deepening and widening of education is the recognition of God's august plan for a nation, and, thro a nation, for all nations. The mind that is at all taught by Christ knows that the genius of His plans of universal sovereignty holds education to be not the luxury of the few, but the right and calling of the many. The spirit of that thought for humanity which Christianity, when faithful to its trust, is ever more strenuously expounding, is the spirit of both intensification and of diffusion. The extension of knowledge is a Christian instinct. The open Bible is both itself a mighty school and is the inspiration of all schools. It at once demands and incites general advance. All gifts toward extension of true thought are tributary toward the sweetening and ennobling of human life. That wisdom and goodness which meet in God are His intention for men whom He trains to know and serve Him.

Generosity is the counterproof of genuine grace. But generosity has wishes that are not bounded by the artificial demarcations of a semi-civilized and half-christianized exclusiveness. Help toward one group only rises to its true stature when it is offered as a step toward the help of all who need help—to the very least and neediest. Uncommon schools are intended at last to leaven and lift common schools, else they lapse into a selfish pedantry which is its own defeat.

"That white soul of my race (nobly said George William Curtis) naturally loves the man, of whatever race or color, who bravely fights and gloriously dies for equal rights, and instinctively loathes every man, who, saved by the blood of such heroes, deems himself made of choicer clay." [1:173] We hail this recognition of the impulse of our beloved state to diffuse the blessings of which knowledge is the almoner and guardian.

And, met as we now are, we also read reverently another paragraph in God's evident method of *process*. We all hope that this fine and well-adapted building will be a means to noble uses and ends, and that the institution it so advantages will 'grow from more to more': but we are to remember that we are celebrating results,—a past as well as a future summons our attention. Here is fruitage as well as blossoming and promise. All survival is proof of fitness. All evolution is essentially ethical in its demonstration that God counts no process too complex, no graduation too slow, no cost too great, no sacrifice too painful, that makes toward betterment. God's way leading up to man, and God's leading of man of which history is the record, is supremely expressive of his will to secure the eventual best. Evolution is charged with ideality.

Therefore, we trace steps, and hope is educated into unfaltering trust that He who sees the end selects the means.

Therefore, we turn properly and heartily to consider her name and prescient fidelity to whose original labors this building is at once a tribute and a testimony. You will I am sure gladly go with me in tracing the personality and services of EMMA HART WILLARD.

She was born in Worthington parish, Connecticut, upon February the 23rd, 1787, and she died in this city of Troy, April 15th, 1870. Her life thus compassed the long period of four-score years and three. It is suggestive of much to say that she was two years old at the date of Washington's first inauguration, and that by five years she survived the death of Lincoln. What events, changes, discoveries, achievements, for America and mankind, crowd the record of those abundant years! Of good stock — that virile stuff that has made the influence of her little state so wide and so enduring,— she was the sixteenth of an old-fashioned family of seventeen children. Beginning upon seventy-five cents a week, she was a teacher at the age of sixteen. Rapidly advancing she became an academy preceptress in Berlin, Conn., in Westfield, Mass., and, in 1807, in Middlebury, Vt. Hers was thus a New England training, well absorbed by a New England character of energy and ideality.

The little town of Middlebury was well-famed for its intelligent society. Of the college there, Dr. Henry Davis was president. Men of Hamilton College who know the story of their Alma Mater recall with pride that having in his hands in 1817 two calls, one to Hamilton and one to Yale, he deliberately preferred the former, and in 1818 as the second president of Hamilton succeeded the lamented and beloved Azel Backus, entering upon a career of fifteen years of arduous and noble service — service whose results are still indelible.

Emma Hart was married to Dr. John Willard, of Middlebury, in 1809. The robbery and the failure of the local bank with which he was connected, led her to open a school for young women in 1814. Avid of books and eager for all mental acquisition and skill, she was also full of ideas that for that time were far advanced. The contrast of the education then afforded to girls with that administered in the College at her doors led her to introduce many new studies and methods.

Great changes have taken place since that early day in the curriculum furnished to both young men and maidens; but preeminently it was Emma Willard who asserted and demonstrated the capacity of young women for higher studies.

Wellesley and Wells and Vassar and Smith and Bryn Mawr are today working upon lines that this pioneer teacher projected and established. Mary Lyon followed this audacious and triumphant lead. It all seems right and natural now: but then it was held as chimerical. Now it keeps a young man well-tasked to prove that he is not the mental inferior of his sister. Then his vanity went all but unchallenged.

Dr. Willard was one husband who took a woman of rare intuition and force at her true value and was his wife's ardent coadjutor.

Mrs. Willard, in 1819, set forth her "Plan for Improving Female Education." To some it seemed revolutionary: but it obtained the warm approval and practical support of Governor DeWitt Clinton, and under his urging she came to Waterford, N. Y. Thenceon she belonged to our own state. By special act, state funds were granted in furtherance of her scheme.

Under the proffer of a more suitable building, she removed to this city of Troy, in 1821, and, adapting the word, established in that year — seventy-four long years ago — the Troy Female *Seminary*.

Her husband who had so trusted and seconded her sound and generous vigor, died in 1825. Her work went on until 1838, when she gave it over to her son and his wife. Thirteen thousand girls, of whom more than five hundred became teachers, received and again diffused the influence of Emma Willard's benign labors. Mrs. Nettie Fowler McCormick, whose wise generosity has written itself upon a great Theological school in Chicago, graduated here in 1854, and she was *one* of many. The true woman whose name we honor today rises up at this fit time, and by her husband's loyal help, this building prolongs what long ago was so bravely done.

Emma Willard journeyed, wrote and 'wrought to the last. "Rocked in the cradle of the deep" was her fine lyric. So, and still in this city, she fell asleep, a well-won rest, in 1870.

Only the Omniscient can measure the fruit and the ever-increasing harvest of so true a woman's work.

Wisely has it been placed upon the pedestal of the statue, today unveiled,

> "HER MOST ENDURING MONUMENT
> THE GRATITUDE OF EDUCATED WOMAN."

Our country, to use her words of 1861, "a continent in extent, an island in security," may well recur to tasks and triumphs such as hers. Not all pyramids are labelled, but here is one that is.

I do not detain your gentle patience with any apostrophe to womanhood. Yonder noble bronze speaks to whomsoever hath ears to hear.

I need not plead for that mutual trust and high cooperation which that noble pair so well illustrated. I only say, would that more men appreciated those instincts of high service which are maternal beyond the bounds of the household, and whose ample love embraces the needs of all who suffer and aspire. Such wedlock is ideal, and, so, real,—"like perfect music unto perfect words." Well might an old Massachusetts epitaph be borrowed for Emma Willard.

> "A SARAH TO HER HUSBAND,
> A EUNICE TO HER CHILDREN,
> A LOIS TO HER GRANDCHILDREN,
> A LYDIA TO GOD'S MINISTERS,
> A MARTHA TO HER GUESTS,
> A DORCAS TO THE POOR, AND
> AN ANNA TO HER GOD."

That one does his work well is proved in that its perpetuity and power can be transferred to his successors. The proof of active life is its fecundity and transmissiveness. No one has wrought fully whose plans perish with his departure.

Loudly does this time of ours, at once appalling and sublime, summon all duty-loving souls to the strenuous and sublime exactions of stewardship.

We are too sordid of *love*, we do not enough give to the hearts of men, near and far. "Mammon, the least-erected spirit that fell from Heaven" usurps the rights of the heart. We are too selfish with our *ideas*. Living is sharing. Withholding is losing. Truth is a trust and true men its trustees. Our knowledges are not ours to secrete and to hoard, but only ours to impart. And our *substance* is lent for use's sake. Men of great means are only mean men, unless they are also men of great ends. Acquisition if it becomes a lust dries up the soul and violates the first commandment with that covetousness which is idolatry. EMMA WILLARD gave. She gave her heart, her hand, her brain, her gatherings, herself. She joined her name with the generous, who alone and therein are the great. Ability in any measure is responsibility. She did what she could. Oh, that today we all might be nourished and ennobled by entering more fully into her unresting and unwasting spirit!

This is the fulfilment and the only fulfilment of the "law of Christ," who "came not to be ministered unto, but to minister," and to give life as the ransom of many.

I turn, with hearty thanks to God, who has put it into his heart, to acknowledge the exemplary service by which this noble structure is now dedicated to woman and to truth. May God lengthen his days to prosper many with this and like bestowals. May he receive into his own soul the gratitude of those he helps. May he be thrice rewarded in the blessings that add no sorrow.

This RUSSELL SAGE HALL will stand to shelter a noble preparation for high and helpful womanhood, long after we all are gone. It will be more and more beloved, as the years glide on, and rich associations gather about it. But we are sure that no hearts will ever find a purer happiness within its walls than today is theirs who with such affectionate planning have wrought this completion, and who now with overflowing pleasure witness the crowning of the work.

In your names, one and all, dear friends assembled, I congratulate these donors upon the finished and beautiful result of love and generosity.

# Ideals

## AN ADDRESS BEFORE THE GRADUATES OF THE BARTHOLOMEW SCHOOL OF CINCINNATI, OHIO
## MAY 30, 1895

THE genial urgency of the invitation under which I find myself in this present critical situation, was wholly inverse to the value of any service that utterance of mine is adequate to render. In this estimate I am only too sure presently to win your substantial agreement!

Not having eluded the request of the honored head of this school, my little wisdom and less wit is placed at your mercy. It is so easy to give one's note, and alas, often so difficult to meet its promise with full payment! To one who takes such chances there is always a temporary relief in that sagacious truism of Aristotle's, "Count it among the probabilities that many improbable things will happen," and for me there was left the possibility that a providential cyclone, or flood, or some other personal or public disaster, might intervene. But, alas! Congress has adjourned, and no other general calamity has befallen.

Once again, having "treated my resolution," I have tasted the guile of a honeyed invitation, and I am reminded of that response to a toast to Eve's daughters, in which a rapturous devotee so confused his Scott and Pope—

> "O Woman, in our hours of ease,
> Uncertain, coy, and hard to please:
> But seen too oft, familiar with her face,
> We first endure, then pity, then—"

Let me warn all maidens here not to listen to addresses which they intend to reject, and *au contra*, never to say No!

with such ambiguous back-glancing that a later Yes! seems possible. For, out of sheer desperation, ere now, many a man has been "married to get rid of him." It is entirely true that "any man may marry any woman that he pleases—provided he can find any woman that he does please!" It is handy to be well supplied with a previous engagement. As many a cashier, so valuing his services as to anticipate his employers, by raising his own salary, has, to his pain, found that reckoning comes with sure and wool-shod feet, so now my temerity and insolvency are confronted by the relentless and accusing hour. In my plight, I throw myself upon your clemency. Like many another remorseful, if not penitent, convict, I would win the good will of my gaolers, and, by decorum, shorten my time! Being sentenced, let me, at least, be sententious.

A shrewd applicant for a vacant Texas pulpit, when questioned as to the usual length of his sermons replied, "Thirty minutes, with a leaning toward mercy." If not quite so telegrammatic, I shall, at least, attempt no more than the relative liberty of "night rates." I speak of *sermons*, and I must frankly own that since my nature is well "subdued to what it works in" I find my azure always shading toward the pulpit ultramarine. My garb of cogitation has long ago been cut with what an honored teacher of mine used to call the "homiletic bias." "And that they knew full well (or should have known), who gave me public leave to speak to you." Coleridge once said to Lamb, "Did you ever hear me preach?" and Lamb replied, "I never heard you do anything else."

For theme, I had granted the "world all before me where to chose," and, choosing, I have not thought to compete with those faithful instructors who have put into the hands of the young women to whom this occasion chiefly belongs so many well-spun clues—instructions which have set the sturdy warp upon which each one now moving to her own life-loom must henceforth pack home the woof. It will be the fault of the scholars, not of their tutors, if the after-work ravels or is at all woven in with shoddy yarn. These skilled hands have attired your minds in serviceable suits of sober fact. Your consciousness of obligation to their labors of love will deepen as you advance into the years where you will find that it is not the gaudiest wardrobe that wears best.

I would that I might utter some not all-futile and ephemeral word for this group of earnest *debutantes*, and for those who love them well and wish them God-speed. To be at all urgent and cogent, to have help or heartening in it, I know that, even tho it may stammer, what I try to say must, at least, be serious.

Youth may bubble with fun: but just under the ebullition, however merry, there lies, in every soul of noble capacity, the range of intuitive seriousness and sham-hatred.

Genuine energy is too self-respecting for trifling. Wholesome ardor is friendly with kind mirth: but behind all sane humor resolution sits.

Strength smiles, where weakness grins, simpers, or giggles, and the palpitating and earnest purpose that alike resents platitude or sophistication hates nobly that laughter which is but the "crackling of thorns."

The true mind, untainted by commercial or social fictions, ungangrened by mere professionalism, loves truth and soberness, and demands real maxims and lofty aims.

Our strenuous time—as commanding and as epical as any that ever was—a time whose crucial analysis and sharp interrogations prepare the way of God for a clearer and sublimer synthesis, for a braver affirmation of truth and duty, than ever yet dawned upon the tribes of men—the great TO-DAY, and the to-morrow that hastens, these summon and enjoin all manhood and all womanhood to meet the lifting horizons with reverent brows and purged eyes.

Solemn issues beckon and claim sincere souls, and such I ask to go with me now, as in the time alloted I speak of IDEALS.

"All things (says an old Hebrew book) are double, one over

against another." Our world is full of an august and coherent symbolism. It is "a copy and shadow of the heavenly," "like in pattern to the true." It teems with prophecy and revelation. The "seen and temporal" is big with premonition of the "unseen and eternal." Every true mental as every true spiritual tabernacle is "according to the pattern in the mount."

Men vary, according to their interest in *ideas*, and according to the ideas in which they are interested.

An *idea* is a thing *seen*, a mental image, an inward vision. It is the thought which all appearance quickens. It measures *phenomena* and thus surpasses them. Action and effect arouse the idea; but it is explained only by itself. Plato, and, with Plato, all who hold that mind is original and creative—revealed in organization and force, but not secreted by these—understand that in the world of being the innermost is foremost. Force and form but translate and incarnate mind. The idea is the core. Purpose precedes energy and begets it. Things are the manifestations of thoughts.

Consciousness is aware directly, immediately and finally, of its infinite unlikeness to matter. Each of us, in himself, sees how motion proceeds forth and comes from mind, and, thus aware of what no sophisms long can tangle, we turn toward "the Father of our spirits," "in whom we live, move and are," assured that

"Tho He is so bright and we are so dim;
We are made in His image to witness Him."

All religion (whether the word *religio*, is from *religare* to bind; or from *religere*, to ponder) is the instinct of the relationship between our invisible souls and the invisible God. "God is spirit," and we are. Soul comes from soul and harks back to its original. Howsoever clouded or defective, all religions unite in affirming religion, whose ground and root is in man's intuition of *soul* and his irrepressible instinct to find its rest. Religion's purest Interpreter—one and only among a thousand—bade the wearied world learn, in Him, and of Him, what that rest is.

Religion, then, is the grand tribute, world over and time thro, to spirit, and declares that sense is but its servitor. All poetry, which is the language at once of intuition and of aspiration, says with that Greek whom Paul quoted, "we are His offspring." Faith (whose inimitable definition as "the proving of things not seen," begins the eleventh chapter of "Hebrews,") is the "witness bearer" of the supremacy in this universe of the *idea*. Faith is second-sight. It sees the invisible. "By faith we know the world to have been framed by the word of God, so that what is seen did not come from phenomena,"—that is, the visible order did not originate from the various appearances which it presents. The *word* preceded the *world*. "Because of Thy will they were."

So, at the outset, we observe how deep the philosophy of idealism lodges in religion. Revelation matches mankind's thirst for "the first and the last of the Living One." That all men "feel after God" is the deepest proof that "He is not far from every one of us." Life contradicts those denials which use the very functions of mind to reduce mind to a "strong delusion!"

The idea is the very *substans*—the underfoundation of our natures. Every act of self-expression is the embodiment of a "thought and intent of the heart." Deed is idea translated, and life is the constant process of turning one's self inside out! Both for quality and for quantity, "as a man thinketh so is he." Any other theory of what man is makes him an automaton or a puppet, in either case only a mechanical contrivance. But conscience, in blaming or in commending, affirms that man is responsible, and, if responsible, free. Our thoughts, "accusing or excusing one another," affirm that we are moral and not mechanical. They move in the realm of a finite but real option. Each of us knows that! Self-understanding faces itself as a spirit. Deep within these bodies sits that mysterious self, perceiving, wishing, deciding, and capable instantly to be aware of itself as a thinker and not a thing. Ideas are the food and raiment of souls. Idealism is the soul's proper and distinctive life. So we were made. We are true or false, just as we prefer, and incarnate true or false ideas. Life is an inevitable and persistent distinction of motives from among the various ideas that throng our souls. The heart is a "chamber of imagery," where we renounce this and accept that. Be the idea great and generous, just and commanding, the man is these. If the idea is low, confused, gross, the man is. One's ideal is the thought which he adopts, crowns, and obeys. One's actual inmost preference and purpose becomes himself. Our ideals are those ideas which, by surrender and loyalty, we wed and cherish. Our deeds are the offspring and counterparts of this inner wedlock. We take raw stuff of impression and weave it into the fabric of personality. High ideals are thus the product of high thoughts plus high purposes. So large-mindedness is necessary to large intention. Greatness of soul is given to a mental hospitality at once eager and modest. It sits alert and gracious with open doors and wide windows. The spirit that would search the stars must live in an observatory. To have the best we must both compare and distinguish, admitting all comers and selecting the superior—"being at peace with many, but having one counsellor of a thousand." The sons of Jesse must all file before Samuel, that he may deliberately single out David. The genius for a great ideal must be comprehensive to collect, and exclusive in selecting.

Shakespeare is the first dramatist, because he is so inclusive. He drives an omnibus, and all sorts and conditions of men get in. From the base and the brave we may select our affinities. The mirror reveals a thousand minds, all the way from Iago to Cordelia. Each of us chooses and approves according to his own liking. The capacity to discern ideals in instances is the test of mental power; the preference of the genuine best is the final proof of spiritual excellence  The wise soul seeks goodly pearls, knows the priceless one when it is seen, and sells all else to have that.

Candidly, then, let us recognize that knowledge is shown in ideas, and character in ideals. One is taste, the other is truth. This is the difference between encyclopedia and Bible, between the science of seeing and the art of being. There are brains that are but curiosity-shops, stuffed with inconsequent and second-hand odds and ends—the pawn-place of gems and pewter, tools and toys, laces and jute, bric-a-brac and trash. To be more than pawn-brokers we must order and organize knowledge, and consent to do business in a particular line. It is of no profit to gather if one does not classify,—to observe if one does not reflect. A constructive character must passionately and absorbingly invoke the moral intent of things. It must not only see how the concert of facts implies plan, it must also discover the *summum bonum* which that plan introduces and fulfils. Geometry is ethical. The ultimatum is rightness—rightness whose correlative is duty. This is "the end of being and ideal grace." Sure that this radical, inevitable *ego* is more than the material things amid which it dwells and upon which it works, we are also sure that motives and ends are the summary and goal of its reality. The word *ought* warrants and inspires the word *can*. Function expresses relation and, at last, the cap-sheaf of synthesis is *God*. We are His. He is ours. Love is the last word and has no synonym. It is the harvest-home of philosophy and the desired haven of the soul.

The mind's eye has thus pierced distances no four-foot reflector can fathom. He whom we seek is not at the other end of the telescope, but at this end. God is not the distant object —He is the light by which we search and find, and the mind's eye is His witness. The soul is in His image, and His image is in it.

We, whose pain and glory it is never to rest until we have an idea deep and wide enough "for all the argosies of object and event," have at last struck the true trail—"the trailing cloud of glory." The intuition of the creature is the subjective recognition of the Creator. It is not proof, it is the *open vision*. THIS IS IDEALISM.

This is the insight that interprets and transcends eyesight,— the illumination of the inward eye that makes one a *seer*. It has been well said that there are three orders of sight,— "that which sees things, that which sees into things, that which sees thro things." Observation, understanding, appreciation. What eye hath not seen, nor ear heard, nor hath entered into the deductions of reason, God reveals by his spirit. "The spirit of man is the candle of the Lord." Its light is His. At this open organ the wondrous Player sits. It is built to utter His music. It is this divine-human, human-divine, symphony that peals and trembles in the Hebrew Psalms. God's hand swept the harp of the heart, and therefore religion will never outgrow those chords. Prose is finite. Realism, with its hard postulates, not only has no ear for music, but it must logically deny both the right and reason of song. The lyrical instinct contradicts it. Both the misereres and the anthems of the heart affirm the intuitions whose hopes even the protests of sorrow recognize. Music is a sublime and irrefutable prophecy. That culminating 150th Psalm, which summons to praise "everything that hath breath," is the warrant of a perpetual and augmenting hymnody. Poetry, which is the twin of song, is the irrepressible vehicle of the inmost life. Idealism either compels worship, or its denial renounces it. Both are the evidence of the unseen and eternal. Only in immortal souls are such harmonies.

In the clash and clangor of definitions, where either rash or timid rationalists vie in vain endeavors to transfix with this logical pin, or that, the elusive wings of inspiration, we must not for an instant forget that the devout heart always knows more than it can utter, and that no one expression can satisfy or exhaust it. It must "say of itself" and not "what some other told" it.

So I plead for Ideality—for that uncommon sense which

seizes the symbolism of the material and sensuous—for that *imag*-ination, which, breathing life into the nostrils of dust, manifests its birthright in God. The commanding reality of the idea sets forth the only plane of spiritual loyalty.

To those alone, who are "not disobedient to the heavenly vision," creation gleams with correspondence and compensation. To such the world is plastic and mobile under the constant energy of God the Holy Ghost. Everywhere the shekinah!

The idealist is no idler. That idealism is not vague revery or sentimental rhapsody, you are now helping to prove by your firm attention to these efforts toward a high and abstract thought. The meta-physical is the soul's privilege and crown.

But consider and know the tree of a sincere idealism by its fruits. Royal imagination has never been atheistic, and under the fullest breath of revelation it has spread its broadest wings. Æschylus and Dante, Milton and Tennyson, Longfellow and Lowell are devout. No literature has been so free and so great as English literature, and none is so saturated with that idealism whose other name is Christianity. Man's loftiest powers have been instructed in affirmation and aspiration. Poetic (that is, *creative*) activity can not breathe the carbonic acid gas of denial. Faith flies where doubt creeps. All noble theory is ethical. But *ethics* resents the duress of custom and circumstance, displays the extra-physical environment of moral law, responds to the fiery forbiddings of an unrepealed Sinai, and to the yet more inquisitive search of the beatitudes, and in the immediate center of human nature erects a tribunal which predicts an ultimate, tho as yet postponed, poetic justice. The ancient reasoning of Plutarch, "concerning such as the gods are slow to punish," still is valid.

The terrors of the law are interior realities, and their upshutting to sheer mercy reveals the world of spiritual judgment in which we already dwell. If we will not heed the sadness of Solomon, we may listen to the melancholy of Wilhelm Meister. If Judas can not teach us, nor Pilate, we can heed

Benedict Arnold and Aaron Burr. If Jezebel shall not warn, Lady Macbeth shall. Remorse, too, is ideality.

Idolatry is baneful because it parodies the ideal. The essence of the "second commandment" lies in the danger that "*graven* images" would displace the mental image of God, and transfer to a dead device that emphasis which was meant to rest upon communion with the Holy- and Living-One. That not even the incarnation of Christ should deny this permanent need, He said, "It is expedient for you that I go away."

Idealism, unconscious or confessed, is at the base of all power. By it (as Stopford Brooke says, in his recent fine treatise upon the secret of Tennyson, page 152), we are to be "saved from the impertinent despotism which claims that the reasoning intellect is higher than the imagination, and the work of Science more important to man than the work of Art." To feel the profound teaching that underlies simple things is the proof of spiritual stature. It is the badge of noble minds, that, where many see but trifles, or see naught, they get the schooling of analogies. That was high praise which Charles Sumner gave Lincoln, when he said that, "To him, illustration is equally important with the argument; his ideas, like the animals into the ark, *go in pairs*." All true greatness, adds to judgment, imagination and hope. It thus interprets the accident by the essence, and so is persuaded of the possible, announces it, embraces it, while it is yet afar off. This patient prescience, this devotion to a truth and anticipation of its triumph, even while as yet it is ignored or denied — what is this but the *faith* whose instances make the paragraphs of the eleventh of Hebrews so resonant and so dramatic? What were Enoch, Abraham, Moses, Job, Isaiah, John the Baptist, and and that greater Plato, John, the evangelist and seer, if not sublime *idealists*, alive to the absolute, and treading the upper levels, under the light to come?

> "Far into distant worlds they pried,
> And brought eternal glories near."

True ideality is not imitative, but creative. Here runs the line of division between rhymer and poet — Pope, of Twickenham, dwelling in preposterous Arcadias, full of pat conceits and adroit fancies, enamored of unscrupulous antitheses — between such an one and a serene Wordsworth, an epoch-voicing Tennyson, or an epoch-urging Whittier. Mere fancy is but a kind of intellectual photography. It fixes the instance but it misses suggestion. Creative genius works out of the particular to the general, and its portraitures are illustrious with "a light that never was on sea or land." Contrary to the frequent and dull notion that imagination is impractical, we may aver that its anticipations of things "not seen as yet," are superlatively practical. Ideals — the stimulations of ultimate truths — stand behind all high performance. Progress is led by those who see visions and dream dreams. The most practical men are they who, earlier than their fellows, perceive what can be and ought to be, and who bend brain and hand to get it done. They are stout to shape ideas into acts. They become the heralds of the future, and across the impassable they throw themselves as a living bridge. Men, "to whom the commonplace is forever unintelligible," resent their message and call them visionaries and iconoclasts. Dastards and reactionaries hate those to whom life means the pursuit of high objects: but these, blowing away the malarial fogs of tradition, inertia, and the *lassez faire* of the moribund, lift the horizon of the world. They are *avant couriers* of Providence. They punctuate history. It is under the contagion of such lives — lives that no coffin can hold — that Froude writes (Studies 1:35): "The drama of history is imperishable, and the lessons of it will be lessons for which we have no words. The address of history is less to the understanding than to the higher emotions. We learn in it to sympathize with what is great and good; we learn to hate what is base. In the companionship of the illustrious natures who have shaped the fortunes of the world, we escape from the littlenesses which cling to the round of common life, and our minds are tuned to a higher and nobler key." What is this but to say that motive is more than muscle, and and that he who is mastered by the highest motive is he who most stirs the pulses and guides the on-marching of man? The personality of such efficient souls is not translatable — its idiom is its own. They do not define their ideals, they live them.

"Consider," as Froude says again, "what the Odyssey would be reduced to an analysis." It is to be felt, not formulated. Tennyson felt the breezes that fanned the Mediterranean of Homer when he wrote —

> " My purpose holds
> To sail beyond the sunset and the baths
> Of all the Western stars. It may be that the gulfs
> Shall wash us down ; it may be we shall touch
> The happy isles."

Yes! Consider how deeply the power of the unseen wrought in Columbus before he placed upon the map the continent that was in his heart! Think what part an irrepressible instinct played, when the daring voyagers of Elizabeth's reign "wooed all the oceans with their sturdy keels." Angelo conceived "the Pantheon hung in mid-air," and then lifted the dome of St. Peter's. Leverrier thought out Neptune, then predicted, then saw it. Roget de Lisle *was* the Marseillaise hymn, and then sung it, hoarse with the shouts of nations, thunder-rhythmed with tread of a million feet trampling the gilded woodwork of rotten thrones. "Ein feste Burg" was the echo of Luther's confidence in Him who fills all the mountains with His chariots. Cromwell's spirit had already fought thro the battle when his Ironsides "rode down among the blue bonnets at Dunbar," and amid the fogs of the border pitched that 68th Psalm in an immortal key — "Arise, O God, and let Thine enemies be scattered." The men and women of the Mayflower brought New England with them in their shallop. Sam Adams loved liberty, wedded her, and so inspired the struggle of the men who "fired for God's sake" at Concord, and at last received the sword of my lord Cornwallis, at Yorktown. Hamilton saw "the noble perspective of a great federal republic," and being dead yet speaketh. Abraham "believed God," and became the patriarch of three religions. Wycliffe dreamed of an open Bible, and made it true. "The Pilgrim's Progress" was Bunyan's autobiography. Lincoln travailed in pain with his decree of emancipation, and then it was born. Bismarck and Cavour listened to the inner voice, and Germany and Italy sprang to their feet, each a united people. John Brown struck his blow in the dark, and all the morning stars of Liberty answered him!

The calculus, the steam engine, type, the telephone — all discovery, is out of the *idea*. Invention is first a mental combination — the thought moulding the thing. It is not better tools, but deeper wits, that explains an Edison. What is *inspiration* but the idea of God imparted to upward-open minds. When, at Pentecost, the power of Christ dawned upon those plain disciples, they went forth to "shake all the mighty world." The sublime interpretations of the Gospel are the supreme demonstration of the soul-sight whereof we speak. Under this august sky man best knows the mysterious inwardness of *being*.

It was when Saul of Tarsus saw what a lifetime of obedience might be, that all his old conceptions shrank to nothingness. All else was loss — submitting to the splendors of Christ, he became the conqueror of three civilizations. Momentous resolution! Idealism conditions apostleship. For an ideal, to be truly our own, must own us. It conquers us into its grandeurs only upon terms of unconditional surrender. High thoughts can not long live in low men. To say, after Ovid, "*meliora proboque, deteriora sequor,*" is at once an elegy and a judicial sentence.

Oh, might some poor word of mine touch to the quick the womanhood of you who now are advancing toward the larger probations of maturity! You will differ, my sisters, in the efficacy of your lives, by just so much as you differ in fidelity to spirit, as superior to sight and sense. It is *motive* that differentiates the doer from the drone, the sybarite from the saint. You stand here now as if with "sealed proposals." Are they noble? are they sordid? Time must tell. Adopt an ambition high enough for eternal character and under it, add yourselves to that phalanx of the eager souled, who, with a thousand varities of task, have realized their ideals under that high pledge — "ONE THING I DO."

Not by exuberant declamation shall you win to the "prize of the high calling," not by theatrical sentimentalities: but by thoughts knit to performance, by the energy which makes its own right of way, by the definitive renunciation of that listless, purposeless existence, which is "as idle as a painted ship upon a painted ocean," by making *duty* the star of all your steering, by absolute allegiance to the "Father of lights."

Life lies there. Will intends work. He who would warm and brighten the world must consume himself. Cheap souls delude themselves with fine talk, but a genuine ideal is expensive. It hates mediocrity. That is a keen German apothegm, "the good is enemy to the best;" for the merely "passable," the "pretty good," the half-baked, "seconds," putty and rubble, demoralize, yes, any one of these debauches him who offers it, and justice wreaks the vengeance of a bar-sinister upon him who shirks sacrifice.

Phariseeism and Sadduceeism, in art and labor, as in religion, alike centering upon self only, forfeit and frustrate that *Love*, whose immortal definition is that it "seeketh not its own." The centripetal motive destines itself to perpetual shrinkage, to futility, to an eternal anti-climax!

I delay you with no picture of the un-ideal life. Place, pleasure, pelf, power, what are these as *ends?* and what are all objects that end in these, but the soul's prostitution!

It was a remark, that seems finer still because Philip Sidney uttered it, that "eagles fly alone." Rarity of altitude—the bird's-eye view—means *separateness*. The penalty of spiritual rank is apt to be a measure of isolation. But the society of absorbingly high ideals can never be solitude. There was one who, in a loneliness of misrepresentation that no experiences of ours can ever make intelligible, declared, "Yet I am not alone."

Antagonisms there must be, and they are neither to be evaded nor feared. It is the divine testimony, not the garnished sepulcher that makes the prophet great. "They may kill me if they can catch me," said Socrates. But is Socrates dead? Are any dead of the "choir invisible"—the omnipotent minority—who have set the share of truth in the fallow generations and plowed their several furrows to the wall!

The very elements fight for the free spirit that does not (in the words of Ruskin), "lower the level of its aim to enjoy the complacency of success." Wider than the waters could carry the ashes of John Wycliffe, strewn by impotent malice, they have carried that open book which tyrants hate! They might impale at Tyburn bar that head, terrible to all Stuarts and their ilk, but the fingers of the Protector work yet in the commonwealth of the world.

Thoughts are bessemered into principles only in the crucible, and shaped to use under the steam-hammer. "Talent (wrote Goethe) is developed in solitude; character in the stream of life." Constancy comes at last to its coronation.

When Henry Smart, one of the sincerest of modern English church composers, lay a-dying, he thought he saw the master of his life-work, and half rising, with gleaming face, he cried, "Hi! John Sebastian Bach!" But to each of us who wills, it may be given at last to recognize Him "whose name is above every name"—whom Stephen saw and fell asleep.

To pull the world up the steep grade of Time we must send more steam to the cylinder than to the whistle. Vital enthusiasms make all terrestrial rewards shabby—they turn fins into feet and arms into wings. In the entertaining miscellany of the older D'Israeli, upon the "Literary Character" (2:20), it is written of the mineralogist Werner: "His unwritten lecture was a reverie, till, kindling in his progress, blending science and imagination in the grandeur of his conceptions, at times, as if he had gathered about him the very elements of nature, his spirit seemed to be hovering over the waters and the *strata.*" Such an interpreter holds the master-key to all locks.

"The lesson of life," says Emerson, (Rep. Men., pp. 182, 183), "is, practically, *to generalize* — to believe what the years and the centuries say against the hours — to resist the usurpation of particulars, and to penetrate to their catholic sense." "This faith avails to the whole emergency of life and objects. The world is saturated with Deity and with law. A man of thought must feel that thought is the parent of the Universe."

This topmost plane of philosophical idealism is, however, but the lowest stair of that spiritual confidence whose courage it is that "All things work together for good to them that love God."

If, now, at last, some of you are thinking that this paper has been too much a homily, and too little a literary excursion, let me ask you, *What is literature?* What but the record of ideas and of man's life therein? What does college or school stand for, if not for the society of ideals and the discipline of their inculcation. What is education but the *eduction* of the inner nature? What are facts worth without this factoring? Your library is the memorial of personalities striving to interpret life, and thro its materials to discover its meaning. A library is an arsenal for those who fight under the colors that never shall be struck. The vitalest books are those in which blazing and unconsumable souls allure us to try the way they trod. The books we heed are the books that bleed. The sufferers are the sages. Their works do follow them. They are of no date, and carry the *imprimatur* of God. A library is no mausoleum, but the populous abode of the mighty who cannot die.

And so, to strike the cadence of this monody, let Deborah's

challenge ring yet, "Up! for this is the day! Is not the Lord gone out before you?" Heed Lowell's praise of Chaucer, that "he was the first poet who wrote as if today were as good as yesterday." The evangel is not exhausted. Time advertises for those whose far-sight refuses to believe that the world is used up. There are to be new Iliads.

The age needs sane and serious souls—men who are not tailors' models, nnd women who are not dolls. It calls from the lyric to the epic. It bids the brave to resent the incoherent ethics of that so-called realism which flaunts its hour, to refuse the whining and suicidal postulates that self and sense are final, and to proclaim that materialism in morals is the degradation of conscience from a queen to a scullion, and that in affairs Hedonism is cousin to anarchy!

The divine appeal is to us all, to own the trusteeship of truth, as well as of possessions, and that with a severe *noblesse oblige* all better having imposes a larger debt of sharing.

The hours which run, summon, with a bugle's call, men, and maidens to match them, who shall put aside the paltry for the pure. Patriotism and faith alike lie here. Here are the domestic virtues, "whereon rests the unconquerable state." Here waits the chivalry of Christ. These are the "daughters that prophesy." This is the womanhood that wears the imperial crown.

> "Then reign the world's great bridals, calm and chaste,
> Thence springs the crowning race of human kind."

Ye "blessed damozels," such, and such only can command the century which must be either epical or tragic. God grant you, therefore, to be *idealists*—and more than you ask or think to have your dreams come true. For the humble bravery, which trusts the powers of an endless life, which surmounts itself in the love that "beareth all things, hopeth all things, endureth all things, believeth all things," is at one with

> "That God, which ever lives and loves.
> One God, one law, one element,
> And one far-off, divine event
> To which the whole creation moves."

He shall bruise Satan under our feet, and by and by we shall be ready to say with brave Walter Scott (great for his genius, but greater yet for his indomitable honor), that which he so simply penned as his mortal chapter drew to its ending, "I think that next week I shall be in the secret."

# The Stewardship of Knowledge

## AN ADDRESS AT THE OPENING OF THE BROOKLYN INSTITUTE SEPTEMBER 30, 1895

*Mr. President, Members of the Brooklyn Institute, and all Good Friends*—The invitation under which I am to speak to you, while it confers a great honor, also imposes a severe responsibility. The best reasoned conclusions, the most compelling sympathy, could not be too much for this earnest assembly and alert hour. I cannot hope to disguise the limitations, which, as I begin, are so uncomfortably real to me. I can only ask of your 'associated censorship,' Portia's quality of mercy.

Only in wakening your self-realization, and in touching, however poorly, your enthusiasms for what this Institute is and purposes, shall I at all avoid the penalty of that temerity of mine which is just now our common misfortune.

So far, then, my unfeigned condolence: but for all else my admiring congratulations, tempered only by that note of sorrow which you all must sound as you miss the hoped-for presence of one whom you have so long loved and trusted as a leader in the best life of this community. This city is at once the richer and the poorer because the Rev. Dr. Charles H. Hall is tonight the guest of God!

It is a privilege to which I am deeply sensitive that I have been introduced to you by one whose station as the Nestor of all learned and Christian utterance in this good town, there are none to dispute and myriads to recognize. Long may Dr. Storrs, as your most representative citizen, receive your ready acclaim.

I spoke of self-realization. By that I mean the realization of what this Institute is and is able to become.

An unconscious sagacity ruled the efforts of Augustus Graham in 1823 and thenceon. He builded (as do all true architects) better than he knew. Your augmenting constituency, now four-thousand, with its still wider influence and stimulation, is the present fruitage of what he planted in hope. The capitoline edifice that is to adorn your park will be his outward monument: but even its amplitude will be but promise and symbol of what none of you can now measure.

Halls, libraries, conservatories, galleries, platforms, chairs, apparatus — what breadth and uplift does your program bespeak! Your scope is naught less than to articulate the whole mental aesthetic, ethical life of this fourth city of the nation.

If you build as high as you are planning wide, and if this community shall at all realize and avail itself of the opportunity which it is your ambition to make ever more ample and more inviting, then this work will have recognition as the most commanding feature of your civic life, and those (if there are any) who have questioned your peerage will praise your supremacy.

I for one wonder that any are to be found in such a population, and a population of such a quality, to hold lightly or wilingly to forego the autonomy of a corporation of such high omens, or to wish to merge its individuality of ideas into the mere bulk of commercial unity with a neighbor which, however great, need not desire to swallow you whole and alive!

Were I a citizen here, far rather would I plead for another star in the flag, for the erection of Long Island into an independent state with Brooklyn as its capital! Between Tioga County and Manhattan Island Albany would still be busy!

But, letting all that pass, I turn toward the things more immediately belonging to my present permission, and crave your sympathetic hearing.

This Brooklyn is not only a "city of churches," but also a city of high-minded men and women, of strong domesticity, of fearless and cogent journalism, of noble schools — a city of thoughtful and representative American life.

You have no need of imported teaching or exhortation. Your Newcastle needs neither to bring in coals nor fire!

The best that one can offer to this municipal intelligence and zeal, can only reflect, not enlarge, your own considerate determinations.

I should be embarassed and restrained in this presence of so many whose peer I cannot hope and will not pretend to be, did I not know that the most competent are always the most gentle.

I have no discoveries, no panaceas, no surprises to propound: but can only seek to be the echo of your own good sense, the voice of sober conclusions that must accord with your own desires for the reasoned good and true gain of this great city, and of all our cities and our land in this decade that runs so fast and in that century whose imminent issues shall be so terrific or so august.

For thoughtful souls must feel that "God's balances by angels watched" were never 'hung across the skies' to measure more potent results than now are to be weighed. The accelerating pace of the world commands our awe. The step of Providence rocks the round Earth.

Esau and Jacob struggle again in the womb of time. Empires verge to the day of Armageddon!

Transient adjustments, and compromises of expediency, must give way to the authority of the Son of Man, and to the arbitration of the peace of God.

I do not deplore, I welcome, an age that puts all questions to the proof, and exacts righteous relations to the two fundamental propositions of God's sovereignty and man's unity.

There are no surds, or shall be none, in the demonstration of His wisdom, who ordained this planet to be a very Bethlehem among the stars!

The whining cowardice of pessimism, and the coarse and

brutal optimism of self-idolatry, with its two insanities of covetousness and carnal pleasure, are alike repugnant to those who both hear the murmur of man's great unrest and listen to the bird song of God's dawn!

The only Healer comes!

> "The healing of His seamless dress
> Is by our beds of pain,
> We touch Him in life's throng and press
> And we are whole again."

The crisis of this fevered world is momentous, but under Him "to whom all power is given" it shall not be a collapse but a convalescence!

The song of time is not a lullaby nor a ballad, but it is not a dirge. It shall be an anthem, even the *Gloria in Excelsis Deo, et in terra pax!*

A child on Mt. Washington watched with his father a glorious sunset as it shot the clouds with unspeakable splendors, and exclaimed—"Oh papa, I see the Doxology." Let us seek the heights where solar power interprets the horizons! Let today's Sun go down—tomorrow's shall rise!

With that acumen which was an inspired instinct the Apostle Paul struck for the cities. The city is the fulcrum of opportunity. Taught truly its cities shall tutor the land. Their salvation shall make all good dominant.

And so in this instant which we call *now*—which is always the accepted time,—and in this vocal city I try to affirm a truth which has in it 'the potency and promise of every form of life'—*this*—"THE STEWARDSHIP OF KNOWLEDGE."

I am sure that all your hearts are keyed to that theme, and I am thankful to speak to those who already believe.

I stand here as an inadaquate but loyal representative of one of what Holmes once playfully characterized as 'the freshwater colleges.'

For some purposes, friends, salt water is not the best. Truly it is an element in which the heirs of the Mayflower and the Guerriere have proved staunch and sturdy down to the other day when the dun raven skulked (or sulked) away from proving the eagle wings of the Defender: but it is among the hills the fountains run wherefrom we drink.  On the high crests of Oneida County stands Hamilton College, little in some ways, but to her sons large and lovely.

In the name of such a college, placed amid scenes worthy of increased renown, bound up with patriotic names, proud of her colors and her story, I speak tonight of those guarantees of liberty of which men educated in obligation are under God the sole guarantors.

For, College or School, University or Institute, the beneficiarys of every endowed seat of learning or of art are by their very relation constituted the heirs and the almoners of a great fiduciary trust.

Ability is answerability—everywhere and all ways.  Private possession, *all* possession is a public trust!  Accountability cannot be escaped.

There are two sorts of souls.  Those who seek for themselves the advantages of things as they are, and those who seek to give themselves to the advantage of things as they ought to be, and therefore may be made to be;—those who accept advancement, and those who confer it, those who would exploit the world and those who would save it—benefactors and malefactors—Christ and the thieves!

A man is "*worth*" what he gives, not what he gets.  One has what he bestows, all else *has him!*  A man of great means, (whether of lucre or of learning) is bound to be a man of great *ends*.  The royal souls are thé generous.  Genius is but another name for generosity.

> "Thyself and thy belongings
> Are not thine own so proper, as to waste
> Thyself upon thy virtues, them on thee.
> Heaven doth with us as we with torches do,
> Not light them for themselves; for if our virtues
> Do not go forth of us, 't were all alike
> As if we had them not.  Spirits are not finely touched,
> But to fine issues."

Possession, of every sort, is opportunity: but without distribution possession is infamy.

He is the true millioniare who rejoices to have a million heirs! Each of us, to the extent of that endowment which God gives him, is a legatee that he may be a steward. It is the common law af all trusts that they can not be delegated. They must be executed or defaulted! In the court of the Supreme Surrogate, many a will constitutes an indictment.

And what is true in the stewardship of crass material wealth is also true in the stewardship of mental and administrative ability. Who can, must.

The sybarite who uses an elegant and fastidious leisure in purveying to mere literary taste, who is dainty in mere editions, a glutton in books, and who in the seclusion of a library ignores or disdains the woe of the world, makes of his knowledge a toy and not a tool. He too is but a miser.

This strenuous age, wherein still the 'people are destroyed for lack of knowledge' demands of us our all and our best.

If shadows are to fall from the truth, and falsehood die, the times challenge and demand souls who shall be filled with the instinct of *help* and wear on helmet and brow *Ich Dien*,—souls ablaze with that love which ever "seeketh not her own," and who, trained for resolute, aggressive, and undaunted leadership, are exemplars in interpreting every least task by the largest ideals.

Municipal politics, with their constant conflict between the sensual and sordid and the honest and humane, furnish a test between soldiership and shirking. The reeking vats of city government demand persistently antiseptic men. These, or the doom of putrid blood! It is by an indomitable resistance of those who would suffer our civil rulers to be a praise to evildoers and a terror to them that do well, that the wicked are *not* to walk on every side while the vilest men are exalted. Sleepy citizens can not resist the sleepless devil. True liberty does not come cheap. Vigilance is none too high a price to pay for it. But it is because those who know are too listless in the doing, because of the gigantic sum in default from those who could and will not, that for our epileptic spasms of public virtue we condone our perennial neglects. "The fault is not with our stars but with ourselves, that we are underlings."

The Son of Man came to break down all middle walls of partition. He shall yet have His triumphant way on Earth!

The Church He established—not the nominalists who merely *say* 'Lord, Lord': but those who seek what he sought for men, *as men*,—that true church against which neither the treachery of false friends nor the hate of open adversaries, nor the gates of Hell, shall prevail—*that* is the "pattern in the mount" of what *society*, in all its international common life, is intended to be, and of what under His augmenting control it shall become!

The instant abolition of differences is impossible—it must come by the slow spirals of process: but the abolition of indifference is both possible and imperative. This, or the deluge.

The true Sociology (and that alone is the true patriotism, all else being insular and parochial)—the true Sociology is an utterly applied Christianity. All unapplied or partially applied theory is but parody, or even blasphemy!

All that is not human is inhuman. All classes are 'dangerous classes.'

If this be 'preaching' the very stones cry it out!

Our time then is none for gentlemanly young women and lady-like young men. Of such there is already 'an elegant sufficiency'—the supply has long exceeded any rational demand.

A dude (like the glazed paper upon pasteboard boxes) is a low grade man with a high grade finish! He reminds one of the remark that 'the Almighty must have a sense of humor, or He would not have made monkeys'! These silken loiterers with falsetto lisp and drawl and hand-shake like a penguin, are a satire and a shame. Sincerity repudiates them as supercargoes and incubi.

Plato defined Man as "a two-legged animal without feathers:" but Diogenes picked a chicken and said, "there is Plato's man." These dawdlers amid the hunger and sorrow of the world are impotents and imbeciles, whom a true sense of the stewardship of all life will shudder off.

Nor are sardonic and pessimistic souls wanted in this God's world. A pessimist is a man who hopes for the worst! "Everything as aint lone and lorn goes contrary" with him. He is of the Gummidge family. He has stood so long that he is soured! No! The leaders are always believers. Doubt is palsied. Its cry is the cry of the barren womb! Doubt is often the pique and mortification which attends the disappointment of an attempted omniscience. Those who best help their generation are such as are resolute to find not the mere facts of this terrestrial environment: but to use these constructively toward the betterment of that relation to God the Father and to Man the Brother, whose last and unsynonymed word is *love*.

"The increase and diffusion of knowledge," to use your quotation of Washington, must come at last to this. "He that loveth not knoweth not." "Tho I have all knowledge and have not love I am nothing."

He who came "that men might have life, and have it more abundantly" was the supreme Teacher because He was the supreme Lover of souls. To evoke and enlarge the best sentiments of men, to quicken their joy by fitting them to bestow as well as to receive, this is basilar in any true philosophy of education.

The increase of power is, at last, in order to the increase of influence. Men are to be lifted, broadened. deepened, that they may not only rise to these larger measures, but most of all realize and prove that they have so risen by imparting their new dimensions to their kind. The kingdom of Heaven is the leaven of this philanthropy! Acquisitiveness of ideas is only a mean hoarding unless these are transmuted into character—

character, which as a 'signet' proves its intaglio upon all it touches. *All* learning, little or large, 'is a dangerous thing' if it is idolized as an end and not consecrated as a means. It is a dissonant jargon of shibboleths,—"a clanging cymbal"—if its stewardship is refused.

Here lies the paramount nobility of the real teacher's office and calling, and that vocation touches its topmost dignity in realizing that influence always transcends instruction and that interpretation by sympathy — a seminal and genial purpose — is the ideal of the master's art.

The true pedagog is saved from the besetting danger of pedantry by heeding that he is a *leader of youth.* Life alone kindles life. Boy or man, whoever turns a plastic side to another, bestows an opportunity that would thrill an angel.

Those men and women, young men and maidens, who accept the advantages of your rare offers of illumination and inspiration are rich indeed, but happy beyond all these are those whom you commission with the privilege of this great giving.

It will be such an interpretation as I now urge that shall save your Institute from the curse and paralysis of institutionalism!

No sordid and cloistral spirit can feed the mind-hunger, and deeper soul-hunger, of our time. The mind itself will reject that which does not use the heart to reach the heart.

But to discover to another his latent capacities of reflection, of feeling, of aspiration, of purpose, is to turn a task into a pean of joy. Here is *wisdom.*

The goal of life is an all-around manhood to the glory of God. The danger of us all is a narrow specialism, a protuberant and lop-sided particularity, a danger which nothing can so well forfend as an early zeal for 'our neighbor's good,' a purpose to escape from egotistic abstraction by finding the lessons afforded in the proximate man. Subjective aspiration needs translating into objective helpfulness. Declaimed generalizations about humanity and the age and education are excellent to run wind-mills: but zeal for everybody is not nearly as important as fidelity to some one. For a world is a sum of individuals.

All of us are 'debtors both to the wise and to the foolish' to transmit with increment the benefits of that vast intellectual and spiritual endowment of which, by no supreme merits of our own, but by the providence of God, we are the beneficiaries in an unreckonable sum.

Hail then to every plan and every task that affirms and maintains the altitude and outlook of such a stewardship of truth.

All good and growth to the endeavors of this people's university whose new year of enlarged service is tonight begun; for,

> "Is true freedom but to break
> Fetters for own dear sake,
> And with leaden hearts forget
> That we owe mankind a debt?
> No! true freedom is to share
> All the chains our brothers bear,
> And with heart and hand to be
> Earnest to make others free."

Pale and poor are all these words of mine: but great and lustrous is the text. Gladly I would disappear behind a theme so large and so alluring. Truth held as a sacred trust — this is the life and light of men. This is the calling and election of scholarship of whatever degree. This is the 'liberal education' offered us by the Giver of all good. Under this banner may you wage and win your new battle of Long Island!

# Ethics in Politics

## SPEECH AT THE CXXVII BANQUET OF THE CHAMBER OF COMMERCE OF THE STATE OF NEW YORK
### NEW YORK CITY, NOVEMBER 19, 1895

---

*Mr. President, Gentlemen, of the Chamber of Commerce, and all good Friends* — It is with an unfeigned diffidence, not to say anxiety, that I find myself confronted by this company and occasion. This house of representatives stands for so much, and its attention demands so much, that any such post-prandial tyro as myself must sympathize with the agued BELSHAZZAR, as he attempts to meet its critical exactions. And yet I am as sure of your generous forbearance, as I am grateful for your confiding hospitality.

A witty parson, whom I knew, once said to a company of theologs — "Young men, you will have observed that all the great preachers have great congregations — the way then to be a great preacher is to have a great congregation!" I would, for your sakes, that the humorous sophism were true. [Laughter.] I heard of a man who rose to speak in the chapel of Auburn prison. There were about 1,700 auditors, in compact rows, all modestly and appropriately attired, and in his embarrassment, the minister began — "Ahem, I'm glad to see so many of you here today!" In like confusion, I can only say, "Me too." [Laughter.] For you are so well wonted to competent and cogent speech, that it is a pity to make this time an exception to the adage that "to him that hath shall be given," or as it was condensed by a shrewd feminine and rural tongue, "Them that has, gits." [Laughter.]

The president of almost anything, is a man expected to keep

ideas on tap, with a spigot for every call. A college president, even if a small president of a large college, is supposed to have an artesian supply of talk. A barrel of addresses and a barrel of sermons, and always ready to fire with both barrels. I confide to you that I have but a small keg and without compartments. It goes on a swivel, like a churn, and is labeled "Sermon" on one end and "Talk" on the other. An address is but a sermon upside down, and a sermon is an address other end up. It does require a certain briskness, like that of the deacon, who, when asked to "*lead*," replied, " I was goin' to make some remarks, but I suppose I can put them in the form of a prayer," or, like that of the Yankee, who, taking a boatload of shoe pegs to New Orleans, and finding the market "long," invented a machine, sharpened the other ends, and sold them for oats. A sermon differs from an address, as a pie differs from a tart, merely in the form of the crust. [Laughter.]

Of a sermon or of a speech often the best is the text. General PORTER, who is the other man to blame for my being here, evidently had in mind his fable of the New-Englanders who "crossed their bees with lightning bugs, so they could work o'nights," when he gave me twenty minutes and all the dictionary. His liberality of permitted topic reminded me of an old BARNUM poster, which ran, "This is the most gigantic, outlandish and unreasonable performance in the world!" "Anything I'd like." It suggests that small girl, who, when her fond father took her to see the new cradleful of twins, meditated a moment and then queried, "Did any of 'em get away?" [Laughter.]

What *not* to say has been my quandary. A man was run over by a heavy wagon, and stepping from the crowd a young mistress of simple surgery, sure of her attainments, whipped out splints and rolled linen, and deftly proceeded to bandage the broken leg of the sufferer. As soon as possible he was taken to a surgeon. "Who, (said the expert,) applied this bandage?" The maiden modestly confessed her handiwork. "It is well done, (said the surgeon,) but it is on the wrong leg!" [Laughter.]

Gentlemen, please remember, that it is dangerous to sleep when the gas is turned on unlighted. I'm much afraid that you will say as did the farmer's wife upon viewing the hippopotamus, "My, ain't he plain!" or be ready to write with the stone-cutter down in Maine, who, having to chisel, for a lamented and scrawny wife, "Lord, she was thine," found no room for the final letter of the last word.

ETHICS have place in politics, because they have place in everything. All human questions are at last ethical. Politics is not the art of office-getting, but is concerned with every policy and program, every interest and exigency, that affects the people. The insisting that this or that tremendous issue must be "taken out of politics" would be amusing, were it not so fatuous. Men sometimes rise to urge that a given matter must be eliminated from "sentiment" and from theories of right and wrong, that it may be considered "practically." Impotence! Sentiment—*moral* sentiment, is the one thing with which all politics must at last reckon. Duty and feeling are omnipresent, and will be found omni-prevalent, because, under God, they are omnipotent. That alone is "practical" which is ethical. All government is ethical, being either good government or misgovernment.

Men tried once to take slavery out of politics, as now they attempt to transfer to some other realm, some no-man's-land, the question of that power which fills with its vomit our cities and our capitols. This land, believe it, cannot endure, half-sober and half-drunken. Whatever debauches labor and wrongs it of the 52 days of rest, ordained in that code whose mercy is written in the very nerves of mankind, is a question that may be avoided and postponed, but must at last be met, and weighted by all arrears of delay.  It is cowardly to shuffle it.  No.  Politics is not a game, it is a task.  It rests in those principles, without which parties suppurate.  Great LINCOLN, with his sane and seer-like sense of the ultimate might of morals, laid his eye, as if to the sights of a long rifle, and said, "Nothing is ever settled until it is settled right." [Applause.]

Last year, so shows your record, you were as happy here as a group of boys with a new-milch cocoanut.  This year you are wiping your lips on the husks.  All of our hats (for I, too, live in the Empire State) were suddenly too small for us!  Now, there is on this Island a demand for Pond's extract, which not even Mr. ROOSEVELT can supply.

You were, then, as pleased as a woman who once told me of a local revival of an earlier writer, saying:  "We had a great mess o' converts!"  You thought the manna might keep over.  It soured.  You did not remember to reckon that with the venal and lupine power which you opposed, one summer only makes a swallow.

Suddenly the new moral vigor of this great City was seized with *locomotor ataxia*, which your lexicon defines for you as "a disease of the spinal chord, characterized by peculiar disturbances of gait and difficulty of coordinating voluntary movements."  It is to be hoped that it may not become "progressive."

Let my poor voice be the phonograph to recall a period from a letter, which, a year ago, you heard with vigorous applause: "Any tricky manipulator or political expert, of whatever complexion, who undertakes, at this date, to train victory upon political lines, to limit it by political ambitions, and to prostitute it to political ends, is an execrable traitor to our municipal interests, and ought to receive from us all, regardless of distinctions of faith or party, that contempt always due to an attempt to emasculate great opportunities by fingering them meanly and pettifoggingly."

There spoke your SAVONAROLA!  I find that MICAIAH and MALACHI, and JOHN BAPTIST and PETER and KNOX, and LATImer, and all that indomitable line, have not been truant from their own times, but have always arraigned the living iniquity and defended the beleaguered truth. It is one of the emoluments of a real prophet to be misunderstood and misrepresented, and to find foes in his own household. It is also his sure mark that not for this does he hesitate or recant. The preachers of genuine righteousness speak in the second person and in the present tense.

But you applauded then. Will you take it back? You cannot take it back. Surely 1894 was not an inspiration that showed itself only in the gift of tongues and that denied their interpretation!

This great municipality is in the condition of that patient, whom, having examined him, his physician overwhelmed with effusive congratulations, explaining, "My dear sir, my dear sir, you have a disease that was supposed to be extinct." [Laughter.]

What are you going to do about it? Relapse into civic pessimism and pussilanimity? "Lackey the varying tide," or rather, say, "Once done can be done again. Done well can be done better." After Chancellorsville, Gettysburg, and by and by Appomatox. [Applause.]

You know the legend of the Scandinavian demigod, who, thinking to twist out a huge root, found he had grappled the head of the great serpent coiled about the Earth. Those are really beneficent humiliations which acquaint us with the size of our tasks.

A man might as well attempt to stay hunger with poppedcorn as to cram the stomach of his sense with the notion that sporadic protestations of virtue can terrify perennial rascality. Intermittent reform is just enough to advertise the business it opposes. Remember Christ's parable of the tenantless house, the restless devil walking thro dry places, and the latter state of the man who forgot that it is not enough to expel the bad, but that it is necessary to dispossess it by installing the good.

A trouble with many reforms, personal as well as public, is that they are critical rather than constructive.  They dig the cellar, but they do not build the house.  They lack architecture.  They imagine that a ballot has value *per se*, whereas it is good only as it is a note of hand, a promise to do.  If it does not stand for a will, a will that will find ways or make them, then it is only a waste shred of wood pulp!

No; eye to eye, foot to foot, must our cities be retaken, as once they crowded back the Commune in Paris.  For this war of the threshhold no "ninety days men" will answer. [Applause.]

I asked a friend of mine what not to speak of here.  I appreciate his shrewd reply:  " No Rum, Romanism and Rebellion, no politics, nor much religion."  The only rebels hereabouts I know of today are in the Sandwich Islands and in Cuba.  I believe they will at last win all of their two cases.  I hope so.

As to the Roman church, I thank God for its abundant good fruits among us, for its increase of grace, and for its present testimony for law and liberty, and against treason and vice.  I do not wish to see it, any more than I wish to see the Presbyterian church allied to the State as such.  Neither could ever be.  Because I am an American and a Prostestant, I protest against both the arguments and methods of the A. P. A.  God bless all who name Christ in sincerity, say I, and give them light and mutual love.

As to Rum, it speaks for itself.  The saloon is non-bi-anti — or multi-partisan, just as suits its purpose.  It is for itself.  It is the great public courtesan, and seduces legislators with absolute impartiality.  In responsibility for its waste, dis- 'honors are easy.'  " Making nice of no vile hold," it sets the blistering iron of its approbation and ownership upon demagogues and panderers of all given names.  I am proud that the metropolis of my native State has at last a mastiff whose bite is even better than his bark. [Applause.]

Well, " No politics and not much religion."  Let me then "preach against the Mormons, for they have no friends in the congregation," or let me rouse you to recognize the unspeakableness of the Turk!

Never did religion, not the snarl of ecclesiastics, but the religion that is pure and undefiled, more need to come close to affairs. Never did affairs more need to be interpreted by the everlasting yea and nay of Almighty God.

Politics covers the whole mechanism of life; religion contains its whole motive. Forego these two and you are *in vacuo*. I know that I am not to handle the shibboleths of sect or party; but surely I may and I do appeal to both the reverence and the patriotism of this Chamber. And so I name the exacting and determinate fact that the battle ground where our institutions are to fight for very life is the municipality. EMERSON said, "Cities illustrate the land." A century ago our cities contained one-thirtieth of our population. Now they contain one-third. Our corporate life is for the most part either urban or just suburban. Whatever, then, blesses or curses the City, perjures or ennobles it, animalizes or spiritualizes it,—debases or exalts the Nation. And in view of what is so undeniable, I make this my main contention, and it is an ethical contention, that national and municipal politics of right ought to be absolutely distinct. A City is a great business, National watchwords bring only mischief into its management. Partisanship should have no more to do with the Police, the Health department, the Fire force, with street-cleansing, than with the Army. This is truism; but how far are our chief cities from seeing it. [Applause.] A vicious theory must be exterminated before the Common Councils of our land shall cease to be the opportunity of scoundrels. Men are not always to be plundered, ring-ridden, boss-driven, crank-confused, unless by consent. This City has reached the age of consent! Has it not also reached the age of resistance? Mere pleasuring, the dry-rot of avarice, the timidity of investment, the dawdler who cares more for the points of a horse than he does for the suffering of men, the Anglomaniac, the dude, (fake and fad in one,) all this and these must be renounced for the sake of a clean City, administered by clean men. Apathy is a crime. The non-voter ranks with the purchased voter, his price being selfish ease. His nonchalance is civic treason. Whether such a clean City can be had is the crucial test of the Republic. The bi-partisanship of setting a thief to catch a thief won't do. Deals, shifts, evasions, must be forsworn. The ranks of plain men must be convinced, and by whatever missionary work is needed, that health, safety, economy, manhood, all rest in honest government. Stern, resonant and incorrigible the cry must go up from this rock-ribbed island, "Nothing for tribute, everything for defence." [Applause.]

Is the situation today in any of our chief cities without shame? You recall DE QUINCY's consideration of "Murder as a fine art." He says, "My face is set against it *in toto*. For if once a man indulges himself in murder, very soon he comes to think little of robbing, and from robbing he comes next to drinking and Sabbath breaking, and from that to incivility and procrastination. Once begin upon this downward path, you never know where you are to stop. Many a man has dated his ruin from some murder or other that perhaps he thought little of at the time." Delicious. With a similar absurdity of anti-climax we may say of our American civic conditions that they are both abominable and disagreeable!

Just now there is a strife of cities, as there was once a strife among the twelve disciples, "which should be the greatest." But bigness is not greatness. Bulk is not honor. You talk of a greater New York. But this City is far more in need of quality than of quantity. So is Brooklyn. Lumping the moral assets of these two towns will not increase them. Mixture is not multiplication. Redistribution is not regeneration. There will be a truly greater New York when there is a tremendous increase of greater New Yorkers. The extinguished foreigner, who, for obvious reasons, chose to remove the contest of this autumn from the good salt water which once floated "Le Bon Homme Richard" and the "Kearsarge," has recently attempted to launch the issue in dish-water. Avoid his way. [Laughter.] As true Defenders of the land meet the race. Metropolitan honor is the goal. Take the whole contention out of the dish-water of partisan recrimination, and launch it in the blue open of patriotism.

> "It may be that the gulfs shall wash us down,
> It may be we shall touch the happy isles."

If we would be no longer underlings to the dynasty of a theory that finds no place in politics for ethics, we must realize that lust of power is as fatal and as corrupt as lust of gain, and that a deal in which offices are the price is as oblique as a deal in which the price is money. Our hope lies in the clear recognition of our dangers, in a deep sense of the wholeness of the interests involved,—in city, commonwealth and country. Realizing the formidableness of the equation to be solved, roused, resolute, angry, it is within your power, gentlemen, to move and guide forces, that at least in these two counties, shall make the antiquated serfdom to partisan competition for spoils, whether of place or pelf, obsolete. The men of this Chamber are able to exert influences that would give this City a new Evacuation-day, and to set an example that would run like the light. The State of sturdy JOHN DIX, and of "Christian jurists, starry-pure like JAY," nay our whole land, would have a new birth of freedom. It would not be an episode: it would be an epic. Bear with me gentlemen, if I say that the hour has come to put all your ethics into all your politics, and to thrust aside the whole rancid philosophy of the wire-puller and the spoilsman.

Love—"love which seeketh not its own"—love to the stout history and providential calling of this splendid City, love to this noble State, love to our whole America, love to Man, and love to the God of righteousness,—

"LOVE SHALL FIND OUT THE WAY."

And so you shall

> "See Truth's white banner floating on before,
> And the good cause, in spite of venal friends
> And base expedients, move to noble ends."

[Applause.]

With gratitude to the Spartan band who have sat out this full evening, I make an end. It is tomorrow, and my up-hill task of the twelfth hour is done. May the moral fast of New York City come to its feast at last, and with acclaim, that none can measure now, the midnight pass over into the morning!

# "Seeing the Unseen"

THE BACCALAUREATE SERMON
TO THE GRADUATING CLASS OF 1893
HAMILTON COLLEGE, SUNDAY JUNE 18, 1893

"*He endured as seeing Him who is invisible.*"
Hebrews, 11:27.

THE Letter to the Hebrews was both an argument and an appeal. With its array of fact and its august consolations, there was blended an unfaltering and personal trust in God. That confidence in and commitment to Him is of the very essence of true religion. Religion is either the fulfilment of a real relationship, or it is a fond dream. The spirit of constancy is so sustained and illuminative thro this whole writing as to make it, concerning *faith*, the classical source both of definition and instance.

Not in any special phase or exercise, but absolute and generic, faith is affirmed as the basis of life and the warrant of all rational hope. The book deals with the apparent vicissitudes of an ever-moving process, and at the same time with the consistency and constancy of Him who guides it,—mutability and the immutable God. By broad retrospect it would prepare souls to recognize and meet ungrievingly the disciplines of change. At the eleventh chapter the argument proper culminates with the resonant citation of preeminent believers, women and men. Certain of the venerable roll are named, souls of altitude that greeted the Sun from afar, and then, 'time failing,' groups and classes are summoned, of those, who, having won their rest, make up the celestial part of that holy alliance and comradeship in which all souls are one who love and seek the will of God.

"Compassed about with so great a cloud of witnesses"— (μαρτύρες doubly, in that they were once the spectacle who now are the spectators)—we are to have the tremendous appeal increased. The clenching thought is that these veterans are to have their work perfected in those better things provided for later days and riper faith.

Fascinating and rewarding as the whole analysis and the various aspect of this great epistle must be found, we are bound now to press in toward that core-idea which rules it all.

What was that "wherein the elders had witness borne to them?" What is the theorem upon which this chapter moves? Why, at the outset, it is given,— a definition which inspires our whole instinct of *flight*, and lifts our eyes past the hills, past the path of the eagles, up the ways of the angels! "Now faith — (and right there the writer leaves the ground and takes the wings of the morning) "*faith is the proving of things not seen*"—the "*assurance of things hoped for.*" Faith is itself *a proof*, a *conviction*. This eleventh chapter is that proposition amplified by instance. It begins at the beginning (as Genesis and John begin) with "the word of God." We know "that what is seen hath not been made out of things which do appear," that is, (as the Greek noun "φαινομένων" suggests), "*that which we look upon did not come from phenomena.*" Spirit and life are behind phenomena. First-cause precedes second causes. Word is back of world. The seen is the result of the unseen. The Creation *is* a creation, and over and thro it the Creator lives and moves, and the creature who knows this and so lives joins the triumphs of such as are here enrolled.

It is upon the thought that our text condenses, that this roster of great and effectual men proceeds. At the point where we station our present study Moses is the immediate instance. Our text analyzes his life and sums it. Unmatched and solitary that life stands above all the lives of the old Testament: forty years in Egypt, forty years in Midian, forty years in the Wilderness,—"*endurance*," all the way from Nile side to Pisgah top!

Such enduring, under such burdens, borne by such a man, must be accounted for! It must have "assurance" and "proof" under it. And thus the writer to the Hebrews (and so to all souls perplexed by ages of transition and mental disturbance) states this epitome of all that Moses was and did—strikes the chord in which all his life was set—"He endured as seeing Him who is invisible." From first to last his life was one of displacements—it was also one of submissions because of convictions. He accepted the loneliness of leadership. He became therein a type, at once of the sorrow and the grandeur of a prophetic soul. He did not fear Egypt's king; for face to face he knew the Blessed and Only Potentate. The "King eternal immortal, invisible," made poor both the riches and the wrath of Pharoah.

This contrast is *contained* in our text, but the very Greek states even more broadly the secret of faith — it is generic not personal — "τον γαρ ἀόρατον ὡς ὁρῶν" — "*as seeing the unseen*,"— God, and all else secured in God, the ruler, and the whole realm beyond present vision. We keep both the euphony and the paradox of the holy page when we say that *faith is the sight of the unseen*. That then shall be our present theme. Transcendental as the statement is, it announces the real wisdom and the real life of the soul. All uplifted and uplifting souls have endured *as seeing the unseen*. Oh, that this penetrative beam of truth might scatter the vagueness with which we think of Faith! It is the vision of the invisible — the "heavenly vision." This "conviction of things not seen" (v. 1.) is a test and organon. What the eye is to sense, *that* confidence in God is to the soul! Sense is not the last of us, we are hyper-physical — we were made to touch the impalpable, to hear the inaudible, to see the unseen.

It is this idea of the soul's true function and self-prophecy that speaks in many another New Testament expression. The very word ἀόρατα marks that great statement in the first chapter of Romans, " the *unseen* things of Him are seen by the things made." Nature is a telescope !

Paul speaks of Christ as "The image of the unseen God."

"The things seen are for a while and the things unseen are forever."

If we "have the eyes of our hearts enlightened" we shall look for the reality that underlies the the apparent, and find that —

"Earth 's crammed with Heaven."

Faith is a "spirit of seeing," spiritual "second sight." Faith is logical. It reasons from the consistency of God. The child clutches his father's hand in the night, knows him, trusts him to guide and so walks homeward thro the dark, and "we go by faith, not what we see." It is faith to go out "not knowing whither," because we know with whom.

Faith is always this — *confidence in and commitment to a person.* Faith is not guessing, it is not arguing, it is not taking chances,— it is trusting someone who is trustworthy. Trust is more than a persuasion from visible evidence, it is self-proving. It is not merely one emotion or attitude out of many, it is a distinct and vital connection with what lies beyond the boundary of the five senses. It is "the masterlight of all our seeing ;" for it is the response of our life to His life who gave us ours — and who made the outer light the universal parable of the inner. Soul at last can be satisfied only with soul. We "thirst for the living God", and surrendering to the compulsions of an irresistable hope we find suddenly that faith is the *guide* of reason. Without faith reason is not a safe guide. Certainty is more than sight, it is insight. All progress, all skill, comes by trusting ourselves to that next step which is ever just beyond present knowledge. It is not as a mere optigraph of Heaven that these scriptures are holy ; but because they prompt that trust in a trustworthy God, which *is* life eternal and already begun. Nor is it only in man's relation to God, but also in his relation to every other person with whom he has to do, that "faith" is indispensable. In other matters also, ocular evidence is neither all nor chief. "Without faith it is impossible to please" *anyone!* The soul itself, and the souls impartiality, count in all convictions. Everywhere we have to reckon with what lies below the horizon. In all things *good faith* is more than compulsion. There is no sphere of thought or action in which it is rational to "dwell *only* in things seen" (Col. 2:18) to inspect *only* "the things before the face" (2 Cor. 10:7). The apostle Peter uses the very word "myopy" when he speaks (2: 1;19) of those who are spiritually "*near-sighted.*"

Everywhere the unseen presses for recognition. Whether in the laboratory, or the garden, on the judge's bench, or upon one's knees — reverence and *expectancy* toward the "things not seen as yet" are indispensable to great result.

To go on from observation to classification, from consequences to cause, from instance to rule,— all assortment and all synthesis,— means *faith.*

The quest alike of the eager mind and of the longing heart is for the ultimate Unity in whom power and pity meet. We are not afraid of too much learning but of *too little* ! The legal cannot be too exact ; and that it may be exact it must be loyal. We are carefully to look down that at last we may fervently look up ! Love is the way of light.

We are now already in what we call "the other world ;" for all God's realms are one. Only now we are withheld from the upper light. We are shut within the shell of sense, and, with sense, can see only its smooth and hard limitations : but we have equipments for which those walls are too narrow and tho now *in embryo* we reckon that wings mean something, and with an act which stakes itself upon the conviction of accessible tho as yet unperceived realities we use our beak upon the fragile and temporary wall !

We are sure that the vast is not a void, that derivative life answers Creative life, that longing is the clue whereby to track love to its source, that, conscience is a 'right line' between man and his Maker, that "the spirit of man is the candle of the Lord," that these things of sight are "a copy and shadow of the heavenly things,"—and so, the deep within us calling to and answering the deep above us, we make God's statutes our songs, pitch our pilgrim tents toward the apocalypse, and rejoice in Him, " whom not having seen we love."

But let us come close to the fact that the perception of that which is out of sight is not an exceptional but a normal function. In every growing and advancing life men "hope for that which they see not." All lofty imagination is of a kind with faith. Duty uses the same faculties and the same methods that we use in all affairs, only the purpose is lifted toward God and the scale prolonged into eternity.

The life of the spirit simply applies to the Being above that which every day relations apply to the beings about us. Civilization rests upon *faith.* Society is Mosaic (a *Mosaic* if you please!) with that which does, dares, and endures, "as seeing the unseen." Faith, as religious, is not different in essence, but in direction. Men who renounce the service of the unseen God, serve their unseen fellows with this very faculty. Architecture works with the same problems whether one builds a church spire or a grain elevator, and certainty as to the external and as to the eternal world is in either case a reasoning from the seen to the unseen. There is no working theory, in physics or psychics, that is not an illustration of Faith. Assurance of the undiscovered—all induction—all foresight, walks Moses' way. Tell me, what other brilliant generalization from particulars ever shot such light on man's mental or moral path as the thought of the trustworthiness, the FIDELITY OF THE CREATOR—that the Universe is rational and not capricious?

We eat, sleep, trade, *by faith.* You wrap money or love in a letter, scratch a few marks on it, attach a stamp, put it into the mail box at the nearest corner, and wait, with a thousand "maybes" menacing, for your answer from Iceland or Calcutta; all because you believe in the integrity and efficiency of the post service. And is it credulity to believe Him "whose eyes out run the morning and who maketh spirits His messengers?" You cable a friend across the sea and get his reply by a strand 3000 miles long, and yet you will cavil at *His* word "running very swiftly" who said, "Before they call I will answer and while they are yet speaking I will hear!"

Albany, and "51," the fastest and promptest train in the world is 12 minutes late by the board. Men walk watch in hand, for they are assured of the Empire State Express. Ten minutes, eleven, and over the Hudson a film of smoke wavers up, while, as we watch, far this side, the train curves into sight and swings out over the bridge. All is haste. Clang go the testing hammers along the wheels. Clank, clank, answer the journal boxes. Couplers and air-tubes snap to their places, and we are behind "893." Tom Dermody, white-haired but keen of eye, is in the saddle there, eight feet over the ties. He has given the cups their fill of velvet oil; and alert and ready the creature waits with strange deep-drawn sighs, the touch of the hand that will hold it to its work. "*'Board!*" and at the word the throttle feels the touch, the mass of mechanism answers the mind that commands it and we are off. Six feet six, twenty feet at every turn, the huge drivers respond to the steam. Up the steep grades, the wheels biting the sanded track, swift and more swiftly past avenue and factory, and the pusher is outsped. Away now into the west. Along the glistening lines of Bessemer, down hill we go—56, 55, 54 seconds to the mile. Five times each second does that piston make and recover its 24-inch stroke—a hundred tons of steel, with a heart of flame, hurling itself toward sunset! The sandy plains swing backward, the Mohawk unwinds its silvery ribbon, the hills stand aside, and by orchard and quarry, thro town and valley, in, out, swinging, sliding, leaping—it is ever on, *on!* What a race! Curving as the river curves, the train seems to cling convulsively to the rails over which it rushes. Can that slender flange hold this awful centrifugal force? How possible seems one mad plunge, with not a soul left this side of eternity to tell what it was like! And, now we think of it, is the engineer competent, cool, sober? Has he good eyes? Are all the switches true? The semaphores twitch to the horizontal: but that is for those who follow us. How is it *ahead!* No pause. Our steed drinks upon the gallop. Rocking with the storm of motion, Tom Dermody peers into the distance and draws the bar a little wider. On, on! Here trailed the Iroquois. Here Herkimer struggled toward Fort Stanwix. Here went Kirkland thro the wilderness and the winter. Could they rise up to look, what would they conceive this thing to be,—this blazing, screaming terror—this tornado of iron? Behold adjustment, contrivance, fuel, fire, force;— nay more, it is an epitome of this strenuous and Earth-subduing age,— it is the transit of the Saxon! Now Deerfield hills throw back the long shriek, sharper than any savage cry of their wild days, and the complaining wheels smother their riot pace under the touch of the same power that compelled them to it. Slower, tho rebelling, slower, and then—still. "Utica!" 95 miles in 90 minutes! On time!

And you submit yourself to that pace and peril, with its multiplied chances of stupid switchmen, flaws in spike or axle, imperfect inspection, a thousand risks to the mile, and you trust your life and other lives more precious to you, because you have confidence in the management of the New York Central. You will, I say, trust yourself to all this mechanism which you do not understand, and to the management with which you are unacquainted, and yet insist that 'only seeing is believing'!

What credulous incredulity is that which refuses to the Creator's control of His own world that which it bestows upon the officials of a railway!

But turn to the market. What is *credit*, national or international, but trust,—trust in that "which no man hath seen or can see"?

Certifications, vouchers, endorsements, bonds,—are these 'sight'? What is 'security' but personality? What were our banks, our whole system of exchange, the United States Treasury itself, without confidence in common conscience?

I say *Faith* is the world's clearing house. Financial infidelity breeds palsy. What is Panic but doubt scaring itself into worse doubt? When but a percentage of unbelief diffuses thro the world of trade, haggard calamity peers in at a thousand doors. What if *all* faith were destroyed! That were such a catastrophe as if the world were suddenly arrested in its turning and all things upon it flung into bottomless chaos.

When relief comes after a stringent or a barren market it is not because there is more money, but because there is less commercial agnosticism!

And here also remember that business credit is what it is by a diffused Christianity. The banks of the world are not in pagan lands. By the river of faith all things flourish.

No more than I would starve while having a certified cheque upon the Chemical Bank, no more will I fail to use what I have every reason to think bears the very endorsement of God.

It is by faith, social, domestic, financial, scholarly, scientific, *as well as* religious,—that we live. Faithlessness is barbarism. If it is barbarism it is also treason. Surely; for how can one be a patriot and at the same time a cynic?

This sixth sense is good sense and no other. Indigent indeed is he who has it not. As the vestal of God, nature lights our way. It is not by observing the lantern, but the way it lightens, that we get us home. He who cares only for objects, and not for the subject of them all, consents to a mere optical illusion.

But I would speak of the *Endurance* which the sight of the unseen teaches and inspires. It is this sight that measures power for daring and for waiting The size of your faith is the size of your manhood. The believers are the doers.

Faith is no idler's possession. It is a high exercise of power. It bids keenly for action.' It is a noble energy of the whole nature. It propels and compels. It is leadership. It is brave.

That Roman was a stalwart believer in his city who bought up the land on which the Carthaginian army was camped!

> "There is *no* unbelief;
> Whoever plants a seed beneath the sod,
> And waits to see it push away the clod,
>   He trusts in God.
>
> Whoever says when clouds are in the sky,
> 'Be patient, heart, light breaketh by and by,'
>   Trusts the Most High.
>
> Whoever lieth on his couch to sleep,
> Content to lock his sense in slumber deep,
>   Knows God will keep.
>
> Whoever says 'Tomorrow,' 'The unknown,'
> 'The future,' trusts that Power alone
>   He dares disown.
>
> The heart that looks on when the eyelids close,
> And dares to live when life has only woes,
>   God's comfort knows.
>
> There is no unbelief;
> And day by day, and night, unconsciously,
> The heart lives by that faith the lips deny;
>   God knoweth why."

It was the sight of the unseen that sent Columbus over sea, that kept Washington in heart as he manœuvered his footsore regiments across the Jerseys, and there was never a discover, a commander, a liberator, an inventor, an author, who was not strong in faith, if strong at all. It is this presentative faculty that has led to all the realized marvels of science. The heroism alike of the inventor and the martyr is faith teaching endurance.

Leverrier predicted and located Neptune, with its orbit of 165 years, because he believed in gravitation. And faith is no more audacious, is just as exact, as scientific, when it trusts His consistent goodness whom all events obey as firmly as the battalions of the stars march west.

Science is Faith plus Investigation.

Religion is Faith plus Service. The sciences of sense or of the soul are both compelled to use the same implement. It has well been said that "The believer in the unseen atom should be the last to ridicule belief in the unseen God." The unseen is at once the problem and the power of all search.

You are more than any or all of your senses. It is soul, not sense, that quivers and exults, moans and rejoices. Your senses are but postmen handing you what they do not read,—electric transmitters, if you please, but only mechanical. Back of these personal being sits, listening as blind Milton listened while his daughters pronounced to him the Greek they did not comprehend. Look! Yonder is Beethoven, old and stone deaf. He weaves passion, pain and peace into strange immortal harmonies. He forges music into light. He is rapt as a Sibyl: but the voice of the oracle is all within. He can not hear his own harpsichord! His soul plays on, and on, shreds of the symphonies of Heaven, and he endures *as hearing the unheard*.

These are the souls that open their windows to the day. They are horizoned by beckoning hands. Strength to bear, to meet and to master the emergencies of life, can only come from the guidance of God. And this can only come by that choice of God which makes Him the first in our hearts. Decision wonderfully clears the mind. God reveals himself to those who surrender to His guardianship. We will but shift our doubts from one hand to the other so long as we forget that in everything commitment seals conviction. Self-will shuts the door from self-knowledge. Sensualism staggers into the arms of scoffing. Mighty faith comes only to mighty devotion. None can teach you *his* faith, nor give it. You must buy for yourselves and pay God's price. The deepest is incommunicable.

> "How can he give his neighbor the real ground,
> His own conviction?"

It is as one who being but a bystander perceives only the absurdity of a telephone dialog, because his ear does not catch the responding voice.

When Titus took Jerusalem and penetrated to the Holy of Holies he saw—nothing. The Shekinah was not for him. We see what we have the soul to see—no more. We abide in the truth in so far as there is truth in *us*. But belief and life are something more than showing that faith toward God has rational analogies. The certainty that vanquishes objection is not argument but commitment. The blessing of Him that dwelt in the burning bush awaits all who will turn aside to see. Self-giving is the price of all high companionships. Hastening into the sweet fulfillments or the terrible surprises of the unseen, (one, or the other, they shall be to us each) we may well quit all else for that which alone has "the power of the world to come."

That sense of the security of righteousness, of the stability of God, can only come by a surrender absolute to the Father of our Spirits. That life of Moses was stupendous with struggle, danger, dissappointment: but it was crowned with a testimony which was also autobiography. "The Eternal God is thy refuge and underneath are the everlasting arms." The shell will be shattered at last!

> Wings! wings!
> To touch the hem of the veil that swings,
> As moved by the breath of God, between
> The world of sense and the world unseen;
> To swoon where the mystic folds divide,
> And wake, a child, on the other side;

> To wake and wonder if it be so,
> And weep for joy at the loss of wo;
> To know the seeker is lost and found;
> To find Love's being but not his bound;
> Oh for the living that dying brings!
>     *Wings! wings!*

*Gentlemen of the Class of 1893:*

You will not ask me to forget that you are the first to whom it is my privilege to say these syllables of parting. I remember it, and shall always remember it.

I have longed to say or to suggest a quickening, and inspiring word to you,— a word that should help you under God toward mastery, first of yourselves and second of your circumstances. The Spirit of your Heavenly Father, the Presence of Him who loved you and gave Himself for you, must broaden and deepen my incompetent speech.

And yet it is my last occasion with you all. Other feet shall tread the ways of our dear hilltop,— others shall answer the chapel call: but, all together, I can never pray with you again, nor talk with you over the open Bible. And for some of us this is the last. Bear then with one more loving and fervent exhortation. In the name of our good College, and by the memory of those who with prayer and toil dedicated its unseen future to the God of wisdom; in the name of those graduate ranks of staunch and reverent men that now are to receive you; in the name of those who have taught you here with genuine solicitude for your noblest culture, "seeking not yours but you," than whom you may find more plausible friends, but none sincerer;— nay, by your own responsibility to your Saviour and your Judge;— I charge you, *be men of second sight!* While the visionaries who fix their affections on this unsubstantial pageant of the senses chide you with absent-mindedness, look you, with the vision of the seer, on into the world of ultimate realities. Put the facts of the soul before the fancies of the senses.

Educate your spirits' vision by using it. Leave both the upstarts who make little of life's most serious and unsilencable questions, and the dastards who avoid them. Let God print upon the inner wall of your very eyelids these words—"AS SEEING THE UNSEEN," and when sense is not enough, when you curtain your eyes for that swift prayer for light which each of you must sometime pray, when all is dark but duty, then remember the Kingdom of the invisible

> "nor bate a jot
> Of heart or hope: but still bear up, and steer
> Right onward."

You have mistakes, and you have also bright successes behind you: but neither way are they final. You may offset the mistakes. You must surpass the successes. To answer the time that with a bugle call challenges constancy of soul and the heroisms of a spiritual philosophy, you must hold fast Him who today is so near to you. May the light of the knowledge of the glory of God shine in your hearts in the face of Jesus Christ! He is your soul's Lord, your Master, your Captain, your Example, your Redeemer. Oh, seize His loving hand! He will stand by you in the furnace of temptation, in the prison of afflictions, in the solitude of responsibility. You shall come, more and more intimately, to *know Him*, and more and more deeply as the rough years move shall you feel that His tender promise is for you, "Yet a little while and *ye shall see Me.*"

# The Indissoluble Life

## THE BACCALAUREATE SERMON
## TO THE GRADUATING CLASS OF *1894*
## HAMILTON COLLEGE, SUNDAY, JUNE *24, 1894*

"Not after *the law of a carnal commandment*, but after *the power of an endless life.*"— HEBREWS 7:16.

It is necessary to see what these words mean in this connection, and from that force to proceed toward the great idea which they open, and which the local application illustrates.

The expression stands in a paragraph whose purpose it is to show the supreme priesthood of Jesus Christ, that He is beyond and above the Levitical succession, that He is after the order of that great king-priest to whom even Abraham gave tithes, accepting his blessing as of a better than himself;—that Christ's priesthood, single, complete, unchangable—is the fulfillment and ideal, which no high-priest of Israel had ever attained— offering one final sacrifice, without infirmity and perfected forevermore.

And this paragraph (and chapter), which, however far away it may seem to us, came close to the daily thinking of the Hebrews who first read it, is part of a minute and patient, and at last triumphant and rapturous, argument, to show the devout Jews, who in those apostolic days had accepted Jesus as the true Messiah, that all that they had loved and lived in of rubric and rite was not now despised but transcended;—that they were not to be troubled because the venerable things of their past were changed; for they were fulfilled not destroyed.

In Christ, all which they had held so intimate as the vessel and vehicle of a precious covenant and a common worship, was not only made good, but made better.

The whole letter to these believing Israelites is based upon the comparison of the old and the new. Contrasts, general and special, are its whole structure. It is ruled by antithesis and argues *a fortiori*.

This our text is an expression eminently characteristic of the argument into which it enters. Christ's place and office is not carnal, transient, legal: but mighty, quickening, enduring.

Put compactly, here is a summary and a confronting—the Old against the New. Law on the one side, life on the other. The life does not deny the law, it surpasses it, taking a higher outlook and a wider outreach. Law works inward from without. Life works outward from within. It is rim *versus* centre,—exterior restraint *versus* interior constraint.

The word 'endless' in the text, is much more exactly rendered, as in the margin, by the word *indissoluble*—a life then essentially and uninterruptedly one in all its parts.

The old dispensation which led up to the fulness and the fulfillment in Christ is set forth as rudimentary and preliminary. It is pedagogical. It is mechanical not dynamic; and so, a moment later, our writer says "for there is a disannulling of a foregoing commandment because of its weakness and unprofitableness (for the law made nothing perfect), and a bringing in thereupon of a better hope, thro which we draw nigh unto God."

The thought I urge is that this contrast between the temporary scope of that special commandment and the boundless scope of that Supreme Life, bases upon and illustrates a general truth of high importance. The contrast is representative of the permanent conditions that divide punctiliousness from power, the narrowness of *legality* from the abundance of *life*.

In all the things which we are saying the chief point is this that there is all the difference between the artificiality of commandment and the spontaneity of life that there is between Aaron and Christ.

The law of all commandment is the law of criticism and repression, the power of all life is the law of appreciation and expansion.

The destructive opposes the constructive because it is *per se* inhibitive and cannot be creative. All precepts are good only as they lead to principles. The literal rule is only a means to the ends of the right living.

Law measures imperfection — life alone can repair and replace. Law may introduce but it can never complete.

The Bible is not only a history but it also gives a philosophy of history and it shows the degrees by which carnal rule is led on to spiritual power. The whole climate of Hebrews is changed from that of Leviticus. This was God's way — always is His way. While at first life, so far as it can be, is stated in the terms of law, at last law is to be transfigured in the terms of life.

Painters and sculptors know rules and work with them: but what knowledge of their rules alone could make a Rubens or Thorwaldsen! The Idylls of the King are grammar *plus* Tennyson. A Lamia is prosody *plus* Keats! The Gettysburg speech was history *plus* Lincoln!

By law we learn to avoid death, but it is by the contact of the inspiration of a superior life that we learn to live.

And these two dispensations of law and of life furnish us with two realms, an upper and a lower, in one of which we must all dwell. The upper includes the lower — life is not *extra* legal, but *super* legal. He who denies or despises law has not learned it, and must, if he would ever go up, go down again to the first principles and rudiments of the teaching of Christ: but law cannot say the last word. For instance, marriage is a contract. That is a sorry marriage which forgets its contract, — that is also a sorry marriage which is only a contract. Carnal commandment *must* be underneath, but it must be *underneath*, — the "power of an indissoluble life."

We may choose, and we must, whether we will live *positively* or *negatively*. I mean whether we shall be *actively* or *passively* good. Whether we shall have that timid and hand-to-mouth behavior which is concerned mainly not to make mistakes, or that vital eagerness which is more concerned to avoid making nothing! A man may be *negatively good*, in the sense that he does no mischief. Such an one idolizes caution until it becomes impotence. His keeping of law is as if one for fear of going wrong were to lash himself to the sign-post at a four-corners, or as if a soldier were to save his powder for fear his gun might burst, or as if a sick man to assure himself against an error by the pharmacist, were to swallow the prescription.

Keeping law means more than eluding penalty — he is still coarse and carnal who does not perceive that *sin* and the consent thereto is the thing law indicates, that seeing *it* in its naked abominableness, the soul may cry out for His help who has the power of the indissoluble life — in whom "the law of the spirit of life makes free from the law of sin and death."

The differentiation of Negative from Positive goodness may be seen in noting the altitude of the Siniatic Law in contrast with the Teaching on the Mount — desert Arabia and fertile Galilee. Here we get right at the idea. The two ways of the one God: but one introductory, the other complete. We may not refuse Him either way, and we must be sure that the primer of particular command is mastered — it cannot be skipped. Neither is it the end. It is much to avoid concrete evil, and so the ten words go on — "*Thou shalt not*" — it is goodness by by exclusion — it is *safe:* but when Christ comes to translate precept into spirit, he gives goodness by inclusion, and that is *strong*. He "Blesses" the humble, suffering, restrained, eager for right, merciful, pure, pacific, — in other words He chooses and extols the life that begins within. Again in summing the law of Moses into two commandments, He made active love to God and Man the whole result. Christ states goodness; but in a new way. He shows how ten "thou-shalt-nots" equal two "thou-shalts." *Positive* goodness is less verbal and more direct. Life advances by exchanging negatives for affirmatives. By mastering rules we grow into relations — we walk in the go-cart that we may walk without it. When the mechanical has become the natural — when effort has become spontaneity, when the crudeness of intention has become the second-nature of intuition, when one has learned to absorb the princi- that is the kernel of the rule — then the elocutionist has become the orator — the disciple the apostle. One noble conformance is worth eight or ten avoidances. Too much 'searching of scripture' is a search for vetos, — too much pruning and too little mulching. Doubtless too much of the education of children says, " don't "— " don't"— instead of " do "— do." The primary lesson, so long as it is needed (but no longer) must be to turn from error; but to proceed in right is the path of life. Preoccupation is a strong protection. A higher interest can supplant a lower. When a child can be made to laugh it is already stopped from crying. The way for a man to stop being stingy is by beginning to be generous. Presently Scrooge is no longer himself! It was because his goodness had been so far only negative — keeping the "shalt-nots"— that the young man, whom Christ invited into the positive and eternal life, went away sorrowful! Meaning not to do harm is much less than determining to do good. The two commandments go deeper than the ten and so at first seem harder to keep: but when drudgery has been overruled by vitality they prove easier — there is all the difference that lies between a balloon and a bird — inflation and wings.

We never do anything right well until we do it unconsciously. To be too much aware of self is to be awkward, or a least artificial. The senses are to be "exercised by use" until they cease to do ill by learning to do well. One must think of the target not of the arrow, — of the bird not of the gun, of the listener and not the song, of the soul and not of the sermon. Medative goodness is prim and timid — it is too self-concerned to dare aggression. It guards its rear instead of advancing its front — it adopts the tactics of McClellan rather than of Sheridan! And still the philosophy of making the provisional seem to be the permanent treats *symptoms* instead of dealing positively and radically with *causes.* Tonic is better than lancet. Build up the system and the disturber quits. Get health in and sickness goes out. Health does not recollect that it has a body. It is when life looses its hold and power that the patient has to fall back upon carnal commandment. A great deal of our religious living is "at a dying rate," or at least "feeble and sickly," because it forgets that the way to fight asphyxia is not by vacuum but by quantities of fresh air. There is a style of piety that is mainly pathological,— speaking with the accent of invalidism it measures mournful doses and adjusts hot-water bags. The power of the Living-One still summons chronic debility and selfish neurasthenia out of itself—as of old—"Arise, take up thy bed, and *walk*"!

It is the expulsive and propulsive dynamic of what is positive that "gives power to the feeble and to them that have no might increases strength." The locomotive gets up steam by going,—the more speed the more draft. To warm a room one must close the window: but he must also light the fire— to raise the temperature the stove is far more important than the thermometer. To get the darkness out of the room one does not use a broom but a lamp. Enter truth, *exeunt* lies. Enter liberty, *exit* bondage. Power is in the ratio of displacement. "Fire makes room for itself," say the Japanese. While dupes consent, tyrants rule them,—not longer. The Czar will take a walk to Siberia just so soon as freedom shatters rotten beaurocracy. There will be a different Russia when there are different Russians.

America will have better cities just so soon as it has better citizens. There will be a morally "greater New York" when there are greater New Yorkers—no earlier. Bad men can be kept out only by putting good men in. That spasmodic reform which stops half-way is illustrated in Christ's parable of the untenanted house—it *was* cleansed: but it was suffered to stand *empty* and so became again the kennel of demons.

Not doing is un-doing. It is content with negations of wrong, in place of zeal for the affirmations of good, that makes so big and so fatal the bulk of *sins of omission*. "*Ye did it not*" may be the irrevocable sentence! He who is either so irresolute or so proud as never to risk a mistake will never do anything. The talent wrapped in a napkin and hid in a hole, hurt no one: but it *helped* no one. No servant will enter into the joy of the Lord by proving that he "never did much ill."

The really upright life must be downright,—willing to blunder *on*—to stumble *forward*—to fall *up*. Real virtue is active—true goodness is *overt*. It *does* and *moves*. It is measured by its momentum. A good citizen is not merely one who keeps out of the criminal court. It is of course something not to go to state's prison: but that cannot be the sum of *patriotism*. I certainly hope that none of you will ever be hung!— but I really hope more for you than that! A Christian is other than merely one who does not flagrantly violate the moral law. All the sanctions of respectability, *ad infinitum* or *ad nauseam*, cannot make a great life—a life of perpetuity. Abstinences from evil are worth while, so far: but it is not the ill we let go but the good we hold fast that 'sizes' us.

The whole Jewish system established at once the value and the weakness of commandment. It was indispensable as an introduction, altogether deficient as a conclusion. It was the preceptor of adolescence—a "tutor until the time appointed." The grandeur of Judaism was its original advance into precept; its decadence and stultification was in its refusal to see how *law* was intended to lead on to and into *life*. Judaism came to worship carnal rule and so at last rejected the vital and perpetual newness of its great Consummator. It learned the letter of exclusive goodness and refused the Spirit of inclusive goodness. It put the trellis for the vine. Thus it elevated the scribe above the prophet and dwindled to a retrospect. The Jews of our Saviour's time had become high-protectionists in religion, and by their very privileges denied their stewardship, ignoring or hating all non-Jews. The Son of Man announcing the ripeness of a changed order—breaking down the partitions of severalty—declaring that the special could only be fulfilled in the universal—arraying the positive against the negative life—endured the inevitable contradiction of parchment and phylactery and signed the charter and covenant of emancipation with the sign of the cross! The monastic spirit repeated the mistake of moribund Judaism and in turn its carnal and perfunctory system went down before the power of wholeness-of-life. For it is the way of life to transcend circumstance not by caution, but by character—not merely to quote a maxim and do a task, but to inspire an ideal and incarnate its joy. This is the freedom of the soul which perceives the spiritual goal of instances and rubric, and (never disdaining their concrete value) holds them always as non-finalities. So does the flood-tide first follow, then fill, and then with its broad sway cover the little indentations of its estuaries. Then the boats go wide and free that at low-ebb must strictly heed the channel.

Ramadan, or Lent, or Sunday,—think how these are kept merely by abstention, instead of by a typical and sacramental substitution of works of love and mercy. If the Lord's day were once used by the alleged followers of Christ in His way—in helping the hungry and heartening the distressed, even if sleek congregations upon cushioned seats sang fewer lyrics in good-natured praise of the cross, had less entertainment in the way of 'sacred rhetoric' with all the week for anti-climax— *that* were to keep the day holy. Long ago Isaiah described the fast God has chosen (58:5.)

The way we keep the 4th Commandment is a specimen of our conception of the others—*not* doing, this and that. It irritates our self-complacency to be told that clean linen and general inertia are only negative virtues and that "it is lawful [the fulness of the law] to *do good* on the Sabbath." Most of us us are semi-Jewish yet in our Christianity! It is vain for us to hope to understand Christ, until we too "go about doing good."

He is the pattern of a strong affirmative, constructive life. The old priesthood offered something else: but He offered Himself. That offering of self is our only availing answer to His call who said that the way to find life is to lose it. He does not now preach economy: but great investment! It is the engineer's business to burn coal, not to save it!

This whole and indissoluble Book is a book of positive and so of profound theories of life. It offers to supplant the vagueness and barrenness of mere negations by invincible realities. It gives us law as a *base of operations*. It teaches us to answer the literature of doubt and denial by the power of Christ. We are to put off the old man by putting on the new, to cease to do evil by learning to do well. Might of spirit does not come by carnal measurements. Doubt dies by *deed*. It is answered by fidelities, not disputations. It is not what we controvert but what we demonstrate that tells. No party and no person is long tolerated whose only outfit is a grievance. "*Non credo*" makes few converts. *Trust* alone can vanquish distrust and "overcome evil with good." The nature and distinction of all conquering greatness is in its displacement of shabby apologizings by daring aggressions. It is in this direction that Phillips Brooks so wisely noted—"how many more resolutions to do right are kept than resolutions not to do wrong." Better be strenuous for one truth than strenuous against ten lies! In chess or in war defensive tactics are to postpone defeat, offensive tactics to win the game.

When in Rio harbor our Admiral manned the guns of the Detroit and said *I will act*—he defended American non-combatants and British too. It was *life*, and all Saxons said 'Amen!' Do your duty and let risks take care of themselves. To live is much more than merely *not to die!*

"HERE LIES ONE WHO NEVER DID MUCH HARM."

Who wants *that* for his epitaph? But if mortuary marble were less diplomatic how often this negative legend would summarize a nominal life! Webster on his last couch said "I still live." Someone attempted to repeat that, and got so near as to make it, "*I ain't dead yet.*"—There is a difference, and it illustrates our present contention.

*Abandon* is the dynamic before which prudentialities shrivel. Personal will alone can rouse will: for, "every seed after its own kind."

At the siege of Port Hudson, in May '63, when the investment had been made complete and the lines were almost within talking distance, the rebels had at one point erected a powerful redoubt, crowned with rifled cannon and crowded with sharpshooters. The Federal soldiers dubbed the point Fort Infernal. It silenced the works in its immediate front and made the trenches deadly. Its vomit of iron seemed as if set with a hair-trigger. On the evening of July 6th General Banks sent for the officers commanding the opposed Union front. He sharply criticised the apparent inaction of the assailants, and to the reply of Col. Berrier that half his guns were dismounted and the redoubt impregnable, the General gave orders that at nine the next morning, at whatever cost of life, the battery should be stormed. "It shall be done" replied the Colonel, and, his bronzed cheek burning under the implied rebuke, he saluted and turned away to consult with his subordinate officers. With one voice they pronounced the attack hopeless and declared that the men would not obey a command that meant the annihilation of their columns. Sternly the Colonel answered them all—"Gentlemen, the attack will be made if I make it alone!"

At half-past eight, of the 7th of July, the troops, mustered close in the trenches, stood gloomy and unresponsive to the words of their commander as with a few words to each company he inspected the line. Watch in hand, he waited the moment, and as the finger marked nine, with sword in hand he leaped to the parapet. "*Forward!*" A tremor fluttered down the front: but they remained irresolute — and there their Colonel, the lead hornets swarming about him. "FORWARD!

Charge!" Heads went down—dark shame flushed the faces, yet still they stayed. "Cover your carcasses, cowards—*I* will storm the battery!" About face and alone! Twelve steps, and over the breastworks went color-sergeant Whittaker, and there were two! A sword and a flag—and the cannon gouging the earth about them to left, to right—the sleet of death pitiless! Madmen, shoulder to shoulder! The fire slackened, heads peered over parapet and bastion—gazing at the two. Then the significance of it dawned on the beholders, and alike from Unionists and Rebels there went up a wild Saxon cheer. It was life! Out of the trenches and over the earthworks came the regiment—wild with the passion to do—tho doing were dying. On and over and in! Steel to steel—soul to soul—they would have stormed Hell!

No one remembered how, but it was done, and as the grimy remnant gathered about the shredded flag struck into the parapet, they heard the faint voice of their wounded Colonel—"Well, boys, you came, after all!"

Fort Infernal had fallen and with it Port Hudson.

*Men of the Class of '94:*
You stand here today with sealed orders as to *where* you are to live and labor: but the *whereby* and *whereunto,* this text, if you will take it to heart, makes an open secret. "κατὰ δύναμιν ζωῆς ἀκαταλύτον"—Power, Life, Indivisibility—what words are these to heed as you go. Carrying love in your hearts for the dear Mother who has done more for you than you now can guess, may you vindicate and honor her by your positive deeds. *Acta non verba!* In the ever-growing library of memory cherish these four volumes, today so near the last paragraph, and of which the whole sum is this—"Quit you like men, be strong in the Lord and in the power of of His might." "If your virtues do not go forth of you, 'twere all alike as if you had them not." Submit your souls to the influences of Christ; for that will evoke your latent capabilities as the miracle of irrigation makes the western desert lands into gardens.

Fidelity to your inmost natures will add your lives to that phalanx of light which is turning the battle to the gates.

The 16-year-old boy who against a field of 400 expert men won recently a great bicycle race, said what is worth remembering. He was eagerly questioned in regard to the way he managed to do it. "I took the best gait that I thought I could maintain for the twenty miles, and kept it up, just the same from start to finish. I did not look at any one, but just kept my eyes on the ground ahead of my wheel, and kept up my gait." There were famous "sprinters" competing with him, but he did not "sprint." The others were watching others to see what they were doing, but he watched nobody but himself.

That is the moral route by which souls arrive at the goal!

God free you from sordid seductions, from base appetite, from the paltry ambitions of the many, and number you all with the glorious few who refuse the sham goodness of conventionality for the tasks and the triumphs of the more excellent way.

God fulfil for you every desire of goodness and every work of faith with power.

May your souls realize themselves in service—

"Like perfect music unto perfect words"

and so may you attain the crown of life! Amen.

# Radical and Conservative

## THE BACCALAUREATE SERMON
## TO THE GRADUATING CLASS OF 1895
## HAMILTON COLLEGE, SUNDAY JUNE 23, 1895

"*Every scribe who hath been made a disciple unto the kingdom of heaven, is like unto a man that is a householder, which bringeth forth out of his treasure things new and old.*"—Matthew 13:52.

RIGHT upon the utterance of several most suggestive parables, Christ turned to his disciples, asking them—"Have ye understood?" And at once, to that important question, he added the words of our text, illustrating how much he meant by really understanding. Therein He described the width and abundance of His own instructions, and so He shows what, in his relative degree, every teacher must be.

He would make all disciples to learn to be such teachers, bringing them, by expectant and eager attention to the sweep and search of His word and work, into the open secret of His method and His purpose. He teaches, as He also rules, by the way both of continuity and of increase. To Him and in Him, time and its tenses are not fragmentary; but truth is a unit, both constant and augmenting.

All that this keeper of His house brings forth, (or, rather, *throws forth*)—swiftly, determinedly—out of his abundant thesaurus, or treasury, is precious. There is no rubbish there—no moth-fret nor rust. Thence we are to accept and adopt "things new and old." What we are now to affirm and urge is the oldness and the newness of the teachings of Christ. He certainly made good this declaration in both argument and accent.

The words of this Instructor of Time were as emphatic and sedate as Mt. Horeb, and yet as fresh as the balsamed winds that blew out of Gilead to ruffle the mirror of the Galilee. His utterances were as old as the light, and yet as new as the morning.

So it came that they who had found the soul and substance of elder revelation, welcomed gladly His authentic message, and that unsophisticated every-day men trusted Him as an authoritative interpreter of those primary problems which lie near to plain hearts. So also those who could only value quotation marks, who had no insight of that which lay back of ceremonial and rubric, who idolized idioms and had lost the idea, failed to comprehend this Scribe of the Spirit and the divine truth-kingdom He announced, and had Him killed.

Whoever, then, (and now it is the same) held to Christ Himself, and pressed past the objections of unfaith and semi-faith, found Him deeper than the oldest words of men, brighter than the newest.

The whole story of that Wisdom Incarnate establishes our text, as the chord in which His testimony was set.

And I go on to say that our Lord's illumination of "things new and old" was not an exception, but rather a specimen of all the normal and constant self-manifestation of God.

The material of truth is changeless, its form is never twice alike. Christ here asserts its variety in unity. One treasury, many things. Let us open wide our minds to the lesson. This heavenly and kingly Scribe is wiser than our half-sight, and quietly rebukes that attitude of mind which looks only in one direction, whether that be backward or forward. For he who but considers the east, equally with him who but considers the west, ignores the half of a complete day.

Christ summons us to live under a whole sky. In Him and in His words, and in those (and their words) who best know and most resemble Him, the past and the present are held not in opposition but in sympathy.

The partial way is the easier and the feebler. The sturdier and more genial way loves to discover the combination, the union, the vital identity of what has been done with what is doing now. For, just as every June is both a result and a cause, the child of an elder and the mother of a junior summer, so, in all the spirit's life, the past and the present are felt to be blended in Him who has "neither beginning of days nor end of years."

Man, in his obstinate fallibility, easily lapses into one or the other of two equally incomplete frames of mind — living, on the one hand, only in what is old, and, on the other hand, only in what is new.

Each mistake is a mistake not only of onesidedness but of outsidedness — the mistake of identifying the eternal substance with its transient appearance, of prefering accident above essence, fashion above fact.

These opposite moods are of course largely temperamental: but it is the business of a rational soul to overcome predisposition and bias, and to get rid of its stiffneckedness by realizing that man's head is not set on a pedestal but on a pivot!

Some minds are eager for any change, and some are always angry at any. The one is born senile, and the other dies puerile.

Each of these classes has its own dislike, whether muttered or mumb, to the under-thought, the wide comprehension of our text. One secretly wishes that Christ had spoken only "things old," and the other would have, even from Him, only "things new." One frustrates truth of its eternal summits of oxygen and outlook, the other would ignore its permanent foundations and base. But every mountain that has heights has also depths. Altitude measures both ways.

The man who loves the old only as old, and the man who seeks the new only as new — each thinks with but one brain-lobe. He whose discipline is unto the wide kingdom of Heaven loves what is true — loves it whether it seems old or new — loves it because it is always both old and new.

There are two words (much misapplied as I hope to show) which in current and somewhat careless fashion are made the class-titles of these alternative habits of mind,—the words Radical and Conservative. Nothing can be more deplorable than to fall entirely under either category, whichsoever it be; for either, by itself, is segmental.

Conservative means preservative. Under this title range all those who dread and repel change, who are angered by the unexpected and tormented by agitation. The conservative hoards decisions and loves only what is gradual and guaranteed. Custom and continuity are his comfort and he is apt to look with a stony face upon the unconventional. An ounce of caution is worth to him a ton of daring. Sudden and precipitous men who would crowd all tenses into the present, who delight in speed and scorn the steam-guage and the escape-valve, who (as Lowell said) "must see the world saved before night," are his abhorrence, and they in turn renounce him as impossible, coagulated, obsolescent!

But whether the Conservative is a dullard and dotard, or a seer and safeguard, rests upon his particular scope and motive. For to test one time by all times, to resist swiftness in the interest of strength, to weigh secure axioms against rash importunities—this is wisdom, and he who has it saves the future, postponing the unripe today that he may secure the bountiful tomorrow. The true Conservative declines both green apples and rotten. The false Conservative, if he marches at all, marches backward. He is crabbed and hard-shelled. He is an antiquary and mediævalist. He adores inertia and is an incorrigible temporizer. "His strength is to sit still." His *forte* is negation. He worships in a pantheon of mummies. To him the present is but a pile of exhausted slag, and history is not a nursery but a graveyard. He likes his manna pickled. Experience is sacred to him as a means wherewith to rebuke hope. He can only accept the prophecies that were long ago fulfilled and the miracles that are memories. The best days are past. He only believes *memoriter.*

The Radical is the man who would go to the root. The tops of things do not satisfy him. His watchword is "*Thoro*." He is assertive, aggressive, intense, sweeping. He nails a besom at his mast-head. He does not add precedents, and he forswears formulas. He prefers any innovation rather than to endure mortmain. Yeast is his element. He rides bare-backed revolution. He wields the iconoclast's hammer, and loves axe and plow and the rubbish-searching flame.

Routine men, who like yellow parchment and pale rubrications and chancery-tape and all that is canonical, resent the radical as an intruder, an impracticable, and a fanatic.

But whether the Radical is a sheer destroyer or a sublime reformer depends upon whether he too is farsighted or nearsighted, upon whether mere destruction or reconstruction is his ultimate and goal. There is a crude and cruel temper whose whole passion it is, not to extend boundaries but to trample them, whose essence is lawless and anarchic. Upon whatever plane of theory or affairs, he who thinks hard without thinking far, or moves fast but not firmly, is a danger and may become a disaster.

No classification of men is ever absolutely accurate. No man falls exactly within a single catagory. But the instance of the partisan who disdains experience, who renounces the sequence of causes, whose prospect scorns retrospect, who mistakes a fancy for a revelation, who thinks his dividend can decree its own divisor, who falls with hysterical rapture upon the neck of "each new-hatched, unfledgèd comrade,"— he will occur under a hundred names. He has his use as a scourge and a warning — the false Radical, who does *not* go to the root.

Of the radicalism of wild excess, clashing with the conservatism of stupid lethargy, the France of just a century ago was a sufficient instance,— the collision of two collossal madnesses!

This then remains; that either type of opinion and method, prevailing in isolation, emphasizes one, and but one, of the two necessary and complementary phases of a full human activity. Man is to look both fore and aft. The best guns are turreted and command both bow and stern. One can wisely neglect neither the synthesis that groups time into a unity—"broadening down *from* precedent *to* precedent," nor the analysis which subjects all phrases, customs, statutes, constitutions, to reinvestigation.

The wild Radical puts out his torch at midnight, the blind Conservative shakes his torch in the face of the noon; but he who has disclaimed infallibility goes, at whatever hour, by the best light that hour offers. There they sit, in senates, or on thrones, robed in the livery of officialism, or brain-bound with hoops of gem-set gold, waiting, or muttering "nothing can be done," the "everlasting No," the *non possumus* of imbecility. History puts them into its museums of fossils. George III may stand for a specimen, or you may take the impotent indecision of James Buchanan. And there too they rush frantic, screaming that everything must be done at once! Your Wilkes's, Dantons, Garrisons.

But now and then an epoch advances which combines both moods. It becomes crystalline and effective. The scarce and ambidextrous man stands up to say, "Something can be done now, if not everything, and what can be done, shall be." With this man comes an era. In him "the old order changeth," as the dried leaves fall before the outpushing buds, while their tree lives and expands. Seeing both possible benefits and possible harms, reckoning with both the obstacles and the helps, enduring or daring, but never shirking, this man waits with a patience that is not delay, and works with a sureness that is not haste. The really large one lays the axe to the root that he may conserve the truths blighted under the rank shadow of a lie, and he also holds back impetuosity, "lest with the tares it pull up the wheat also."

In writing upon the Long Parliament, (1:98), Macaulay has a terse and balanced paragraph upon this matter, and he concludes—"In the sentiments of both classes there is something to approve. But of both the best specimens will be found not far from the common frontier."

Truly it is not in the frigid zone nor the torrid, but in the temperate that the greatest events issue and endure. But, that being said, it is not for dawdlers and sybarites to estimate the stern resolve of an Elijah fronting Jezebel, of Elizabeth's son denouncing Herodias, of Savonarola, and Beza, and Knox, and Samuel Adams, and Phillips, and Sumner. Time-servers cannot realize the indelible influences of the commonwealth of Cromwell, nor can tuft-hunters perceive that he was England's truest king. When such deputy-sheriffs of Almighty God utter their summons let men listen. "So shall He startle many nations." "Kings shall shut their mouths at Him." These radicals are conservative too, tho in a way no small calipers can measure. But in a range far above these stand the calm, comprehensive souls, who know how to work while waiting and wait while working, and their appealing eyes, look past the hour and the event, for the verdict of God. Plato and Tacitus and the nameless writer of the book of Job stand there. There are Angelo and Kepler. There, silent, tender, time-abiding, upon a pedestal cut from the core of things, which no man manufactured and no man can mar, Lincoln stands.

The spherical man is he who beyond the symbol seeks the essence,—who will have that, cost how it may, and will at any cost keep it.

Supreme herein is He upon whose lips absolute righteousness and everlasting peace kissed each other, and to Him,—whether we would dare or endure, pity or denounce, cut down or build up,—to Him we turn for the complete example of the symmetrical life—the life in which all the traits of nobility are coordinate and entire, in which wisdom is not cold nor zeal roiled. And he who would follow Him, must be a manifold man, Conservative and Radical in one.

Under the domain and dominion of Christ, the old and the new, instead of warring, *wed*. Judgment replaces and enthusiasm restores.

The two terms we are discussing are not absolute, but relative. That is but a so-called conservatism, not really such, which mistakes routine associations for the truth itself and identifies the treasure with the earthen vessel,— which prefers an empty ark to a living Messiah.

The true conserver is a Radical, in desiring to keep the real thing. The perennial second commandment is dearer to him than any transient device. Form is to him a utility and life alone is holy. He would preserve what is older than all form in any form that will hold it and would rather have a quart of truth in a square cup than a pint of truth in a round one. Christ was such. His *balance* was far superhuman. He whipped the traffickers from the temple, yet predicted that temples overthrow. He rebuked petrified tradition, yet declared, "I came not to to destroy but to fulfil." To the Pharisees He seemed a rash leveller, to the Herodians a futile moralist. His very disciples often wanted to hasten or to restrain Him: but He would neither hurry nor delay.

He came to 'set men at variance,' to 'kindle a fire,' to 'send a sword,' to say "every plant that My Father hath not planted shall be rooted up," " he that is not for us is against us": but, and also, He considered the bruised reed-pen, and the smouldering flax-wick, the little ones, the lost sheep, and turning pride upside down, He put in the beatitudes a premium upon what the world despises, and He said " he that is not against us is on our part." Evolution and revolution wrought together. Positive yet patient, daring yet cautious, never hedging and never hasting, He was outwardly all that men did not expect and would not comprehend, and inwardly all that they needed. He never snarled and he never sneered. He never mitigated His meaning nor receded from his program.

He affirmed principles and left them to work out their applications. He was too slow for some and too swift for others — bi-partisanship scouted him. He was so supreme that no one measured Him. President Hyde well says, "the average good

man is equally at war with the bad man who is below him and
the progressively good man who is above him. The reformer
and the criminal are about eqnally obnoxious to the man of
*average* goodness and intelligence. The prophets and the be-
trayers are equally odious and promiscuously stoned. The
Saviour is crucified between two thieves."

Still the church is but semi-christian in its emancipation
from what is seen and temporary. It still but begins to know
its mission as Christ's ideal of society. We fail to see that the
husk is precious only for the kernel's sake, and that when the
wheat is gone what is left is straw and chaff. The old is good
while it covers and contains the new, after that it is a dry pod.

John the Baptist was one mighty radical who illustrated the
law that they who wield sharp tools must feel them: but that
axe of his laid to the upas-tree of hollow words was the recon-
structive agent the time was most in need of, and his lonely
voice was the herald of Israel's King.

Every great preserver is called a deformer till he is gone.
Men are prone to garnish the sepulchers of their prophets
with epitaphs: but the prophets with epithets. The many feel
more secure when those who compel them to think are under
a good-sized slab!

It remains for us, if we would neither tear nor raffle this
seamless text, to hold to the fluidity of God's purpose and
providence, and to see the sacredness of all its conduits
whether present or past. They are neither identical nor independent. Truth is perennial, and we hold what we have of it
both as the heirs of our parents and as the trustees of our
children.

That age is most important which does the most to emphasize what is of permanent importance. The wise man perceives both what is permanent and what is progressive, neither
unduly preponderating. The new and the old do not impeach
one another. Origins, means, and ends—all are coordinate.
Revelation is a process by which what is vital and seminal

constantly adapts and enlarges its new expressions. Finality is death, and prejudice the rigor mortis.

'Providence unfolds the book.' It is not a kaleidoscope for a toy, but a telescope for a tool, and it looks deeper than any of us is aware.

Christ planted a thousand seeds that now are forests. Under that Argus-eyed, Atlas-shouldered, Briareus-handed leader both the intensive and the extensive life find scope. Under that calm and conquering dominion we are not to be terrified at ideas that surpass and supersede our inherited schemes. One could not, for instance, crowd our modern (and still tentative) conception of missionary duty into the ideals of the eighteenth century.

Slavery, feudalism, the serfdom of one sex, have felt the touch of Christ's sceptre, and the cowardice of wealth, as the envy of want—all usages without reason, are yet to own His ever germinal Kingdom.

We are to imitate faith (fidelity), not fashions. As our forbears did, so must we,— tell what we learn of God in our own words! We must mint our own coin-current. We are not invited to repeat the wile of the Gibeonites (Joshua 9th) and provide ourselves with what is dry and mouldy! Miracles are not repeated, greater ones are wrought. He who accustoms himself to God's Spirit finds the old renewed in larger wonders. God's latency is all in all. He does not exhaust. Life is incessant innovation. It is only when one stops going that his horizon and perspectives no longer change. "*Tempora non animnm*"—"They change their skies but not their souls who traverse the ocean." New seas are sailed under new stars. It is not the familiar scene but the intimate companion that makes life's journey serene. If you are scholars of the great Teacher, He will give you both review lessons and advance, and, outgrowing your garments, you will find that your apprehension of today will not fit you tomorrow, certainly not the day after tomorrow. " Remember Lot's wife!"

We are put by our God into a day that forces us upon Him. Much does our Lord's word apply to our very time. It is a strong detergent to "every disciple unto the kingdom of Heaven."

The giant is out of the bottle! The era of analysis is not accidental, it is providential. Man needed it. The church needed it. God awakens us from "opiate of usage." It is a revival. The ages in which the status is unchanged are wintry ages. In scholarship, legislation, society, religion, the motionless times are the moribund. Life must either be moribund or more abundant!

A time like our own is deplored by those who dread any change and adored by those who love all change: but, if sane, we will neither neglect nor abuse its disciplines. We may neither surrender to every challenge, nor reject every claim. Truth is not shaken by either assault or doubt. We can do nothing against it. *Magna et prevelabit*—spite of harsh attack or feeble defense.

Just as to a man walking too fast upon a city's crowded sidewalk, every other man is too slow, and to a man walking too slowly every other man is too fast, so the pace of the world is a limitation which we can somewhat affect, but to which, to affect it, we must somewhat conform. We are to advance, if effectively, neither too slowly nor too fast. We are to have to utter new things and old, old things and new. The web if unfolded will show that every true age has pressed home new woof upon the old warp. We cannot do more than to utter our own convictions, and we may not dare do less, both aggressive and circumspect, neither timid nor tumid.

The processes of readjustment compel the processes of restatement, and both these processes come often with clamor and always with pain: but only those wring their hands whose assurances are outside of God. There are half-men, who only see one way, and there are ages dominated by such men that are only half-ages; but the whole man, and so the whole age, looks both ways, and sailing by the North star, or by the Southern Cross, is piloted by Him who sees all and will show all. Holding to Him the genuine soul can never shiver nor shrink.

What we all need is less anxiety over precedent and more confidence in God. In the trust that history is prophecy—that God is here—that He still steers the world, the deep seers of our century have spoken. "In Memoriam" voices this. Whittier is the bard of "that great law, which makes the past time serve today."

> "Whate'r of good the old time had
> Is living still.   *   *   *
> God works in all things. All obey
> His first propulsions from the night.
> Ho, wake and watch! The world is grey
> With morning light."

Wordsworth and Robert Browning are such poet-seers.

No, "this is not our rest" for body or mind. We are *in transitu*. Our souls are under marching orders, and lodge only in tents.

What this word of Christ should fix in us is that truth is eternally young. Revelation, nature, man, providence, yield perpetual increase. The encyclopedia of knowledge must be supplemented with annual volumes.

Pondering the inexhaustibleness of the treasures of God hid in Christ, richer, deeper, wider, with every practical test of them, a truly reverent philosophy of this world, as His, must take on continually grander proportions, and must speak with ever mightier convictions and ever better arguments.

No true science remains stationary. Geology, chemistry, astronomy, biology,— even history,— what changes of method and result have these undergone in three generations! But the objects have not changed, nor have the necessary mathematics of thought changed.

World and event prove Him the Interpreter of time and

eternity. The more He does, the more He both displays and
confirms. His words are not Dead Seas: but wells of living
waters. The "Heir of all things." His latest words are His
largest. Who shall debar His illimitable and crescent sway!
Upon Him all converges, and from Him all radiates. The old
and the new blend in Him.

May every one of us be a true disciple to that kingdom
where the old story bursts into the new song!

*Men of the Class of '95:*

This 'commencement' is an ending: but far more is it a beginning. Poetic fitness, as well as convenience, long ago
transferred it from the autumn of the college year to the summer. Your real curriculum is not behind you, but before.

You are now to translate and parse that "*Sunt quos curri-
culo pulverem Olympicum Collegisse juvat.*" The Olympic
dust is yonder. The college has been but your introduction
to the "*collegisse.*" You are whirling up to the line, and are
all but ready for the word. Let me add my voice to the send-
ing cheer.

When you come panting and straining to the finish—"the
goal nicely-avoided by the glowing wheels, and the noble
palm"—the voices that shout "Well done!" will not sound
here! In that eternal commencement, having "finished your
course with joy," may it be true of you each and all, in a far
deeper sense than bilthe Horace ever considered—"*evehit
ad Deos!*" Bethink yourselves that you are charioteers—"a
θέατρον to the universe and to angels." I am sure that you
would admonish the new-fledged Sophomores here who are
kindly translating my little Latin to the maidens beside them—
("*junctacque Nymphis gratiæ decentes*")— to bestir themselves even already for that third summer hence when they too
shall gather taut the reins for their life race.

Goodbys are always trite: but not the less are they solemn.
Already, to two of your company— to Frank Burrowes, who

died in September, '93, and to John Myers, jr., who died in July, '94,—you have given the irrevocable farewell. Forty-six men began the work of your class four years ago, twenty-nine men complete the roll now. Never, after this week, will so many of you gather under one roof! In groups you will return to the dear hillside of your common love: but little by little your ranks will gather closer, until, perhaps in 1955, you will hold your last class meeting—of one! He will come, the relic of you all. He will ride up the hill he can then no longer climb. He will, with some young guide, not to be born for thirty years yet, observe the stately new buildings, and people the old with you and your comrades of the moss-grown 19th century. Perhaps he will say a kindly word at the mound where one shall be resting who for three years (under whatever college vicissitudes) was a good friend of '95. He will look out upon the lovely slopes, and beyond the curving hills —the boys will gather in their caps and gowns, and cheer,—

*Boom Rah! Boom Rah! Who is he?*
*Vive La! Vive La! XCV!*

—and then—he will go down into the valley!

But in between this day and that work lies—your real standing is to be registered. It is a good time to live! Live well! Live boldly! We shall watch you from this signal station. You will be welcomed back, with your honors new and old. The white spire and its far-flashing point will guide you home again. The bell will greet you. The old well will bubble for you. You will send on your boys for the nineteen-twenties. All good to you in the strenuous years upon which you enter. Be Christ's men! Accept every one of you His name, His present guerdon of self-sacrifice, and graduate having at last "having obtained the good degree," and all of you with high honor!

And this be our goodby.

# Creeds

## THE ANNUAL SERMON BEFORE THE ALUMNI OF AUBURN THEOLOGICAL SEMINARY
### MAY 9, 1895

"*For we know in part.*"—1 Corinthians 13:9.

NEITHER agnosticism nor omniscience! We at once know and do not know; we know something, not everything. According to our knowledge we are to "prophecy," or proclaim. Our present degree is at once a mighty incentive to speech, and a limitation to make reason modest. We are not to be irresolute, and neither are we to assume to be infallible. Energy is our duty, but finality belongs to God.

The Apostle Peter left this catholic admonition: "Grow in grace and in knowledge." These growths, if they are genuine, are coincident. Growth is the proof of life. But growth means outgrowth—not by loss but by gain, by comprehension. The measure of every spiritual soul must be followed by the plus sign. While the present is stated, it is already past. The links of life are an endless and increasing series. "Tomorrow shall (under God) be as today and more abundantly;" the latest the largest; the best wine last. God's "increasing purpose" leads the ductile mind into ever 'more stately mansions.' "For we know in part." And to know that we know in part is the condition of knowing more. It puts us safe from both immobility and confusion.

With the hope that you will open your hearts to this quickening thought, I ask you to reckon with its bearings upon the unclosed question of Creeds.

Fellow Alumni of Auburn, we are children of a school whose genius is that of both conservatism and freedom. This place is not noted either for toadstools or for trilobites. We stand solidly for truth and for valid tests of it and for all of both truth and test that we can get. You will hear me patiently and candidly, as I submit my thesis to your sober and devout consideration.

I, for my part, am sure that one who would appreciate "the law of the spirit of life in Jesus Christ" as a law of progress in both appreciation and affirmation, must renounce that mental inertia and laziness whose indulgence dishonors "the abundance of revelations." Lazy thought is always sleazy thought.

Every man must earn his theological assets, and in his own idiom declare his own conviction. Faith and the hope it nourishes are what none can lend and none borrow. Love's intuitions come at love's price. "Sayest thou this of thyself, or did some others tell it thee of me?" "It is the heart," said Henry B. Smith, "that makes the theologian," and the heart is never satisfied with "the things that are behind." And so it yearns toward the unretracted pledge of our Lord: "Ye shall see greater things than these." Expectancy is cardinal. To regard the tuition of the Eternal Spirit as a closed canon denies the immanence of Christ and regards revelation as a mathematical crystal, rather than as a palpitating heart.

To "know as we ought to know," is to watch the bearings of the figures upon that growing web, upon whose unbroken warp manifold wisdom smites home the woof of the present. These nineteen centuries are not fringe; they are part of the pattern. Providence is the interpreter. Deeper and deeper strike the roots, as the boughs spread wider and wider. The perpetual Leader "takes the things of Christ" and shows their unremitting increase. Far from being orthodox, it is not even devout not to expect new demonstrations of Christ in the application of His exhaustless precepts to new problems. So far we have seen "but a part of his ways, and many such things are with Him." Discipleship can never be stationary. Living waters run. Revelation is not a pond but a stream.

No one transcript says the last word concerning the disclosures of God. Eternity will be forever new with discoveries. Not only are we now, but we will always be under the dawn. Time and Earth speed to their afternoon; but knowledge is a morning whose sun shall rise while God lives. The desiring heart bounds with joy to know that holy and ardent curiosity shall never weary or want, and that love shall never climb its last summit nor utter its last surprised rapture of adoration.

These holy books are not only supremely important history, they are also specimens of God's method — of His continuity of increase.

Everything that is here was first written upon human souls. The book is the corollary of that. The inspiration preceded the record. The parchments were memoranda of God's personal imprimatur upon persons — spirit answering to spirit, the deep within calling to the deep above.

Progress of teaching is displayed from the earliest leaf of scripture to the latest, and the history of doctrine in the church is full of new and newer apprehension of this living oracle. That the book is God's book is shown in that we never learn the last of it. And that the real church is God's church is shown in that it is a school whence no true pupil ever graduates. The 'songs of degrees' will have no end.

Theology is man's philosophy about God. It takes this book of the ages and rearranges its materials into other octavos. It fuses these ores and coins them under its own date. It is an excellent, indeed an indispensable process and result; but not being infallible, it cannot be final. Each new volume grows out of, and is, more or less consciously, educed by the special exigencies and needs of that time that writes it.

Each age is a crucible, and while the mold is provisional and transitional, the material is the main thing. The book is needed, is written, is read and goes to its quiet shelf. It does its work for its own period and whatever is essential has its vital result in the souls of men, there and nowhere else to live. Every statement of truth is good, when it makes the way for one that is better.

I am well aware of its perverse use by some, but nevertheless, I am willing to say with emphasis those lines of England's greatest laureate:

> "Our little systems have their day,
> They have their day and cease to be,
> They are but broken lights of Thee,
> And Thou, O Lord, art more than they."

At once with the systematization of our present, and therefore partial, knowledge, we have introduced a new arrangement. The scientific method has displaced the natural and vital. The sphere has become a cube. It is the problem of squaring the circle. Each new pen adds new figures to the statement. They may and should increase the approximation; but the fraction, however far extended from the decimal point, can never be completed. The scientific method is of indisputable value, but only when its limitations are recognized, when the evidential never usurps the intuitional. It is corroborative, but it is indirect. Fallible hands always wield fallible instruments. Theology is, I gladly consent, "the queen of sciences," but knowledge is the king. He who really knows a thing, knows more than he can scientifically demonstrate.

The inherent danger of systematic theology is rationalism. I do not say the vice, I say the danger. The danger only becomes a vice when we deny or forget it. Rationalism is the vanity of human logic, declaring itself independent and all-sufficing. Orthodox speculation may be, and so far as its manner goes, often is just as rationalistic as heretical speculation.

Our tools are not exact enough so to square the ends of our propositions that we can pile them indefinitely. Just because of our confidence in Biblical premises, we must take as tentative, the conclusions that mix them with our minor premises.

Deduction is insecure after it builds past two or three stories. I prefer to dwell on the ground floor; upon "the things that cannot be shaken." The sorites is man-made. To say more than God is as great heresy as to say less.

The Bible contains doctrine, but it is not a system of doctrine. If it is a system, then any other system is impertinent. I believe the Bible warrants systems of doctrine; but that the quarry is God's and their architecture ours.

Two buildings may honestly try to build in all their materials: but one will be Roman, and another Greek, and others still, Gothic, or modern English. Each may be a mental shelter, none exhausts possibility of combination. A map of the White Mountains from Mt. Washington will be one map, from Mt. Jefferson another. Each will be true if it includes all it can see. The Bible is not a map, it is a mountain range. The maps help to describe the hills; but the hills are the end, and the maps, means. The vital ways of revelation are not mechanical, nor yet metaphysical. The apostles taught and wrote most naturally, not in the way of legal treatise or contract. They were direct rather than diplomatic, narrative rather than discursive. Their ardor was not on the defensive, and their very unguardedness was convincing. Their accuracy surpassed all verbalism, and their harmony was concord rather than unison. They are not collusive, but complemental. And so they are to be taken breadthwise and lifewise. To seize "the analogy of the faith;" both as to method and as to matter, we must take it as they gave it, straining nothing to fit into a "scheme," and contented with Paul to "know in part." This and this only, is to magnify God's word above man's. "Many other things did Jesus which are not written in this book," and I suppose we all adoringly avow that He is still doing. Good faith denies that there is such a thing as profane history; all history is sacred save to profane men.

Biblical Theology, in distinction from Systematic Theology, keeps close to the sources. The Bible is the referee; back and ever back "to the law and the testimony." All books are good that bend to this "Divine Library," as Jerome called it. The technical method of definition is, in terms, finite. It shuts out, as well as shuts in. A fence has necessary uses; sometimes even a barbed-wire fence. It restrains beasts and makes a good roost for birds. For men it should have plenty of gates in it, swinging easily both ways, seeing that in the matter of truth God alone has eminent domain. "Easement" is public right.

Reverence for God's demonstrations, which are truly biological rather than morphological, which in all fulness took the nature of man as their elect vehicle,— this reverence, refusing to be wise above what He says and does, accepts the human paraphrase as partial and evanescent. The seal of our Presbyterian part of God's church is an open Bible. Let it be opened wider, and let our spirits open toward it, always remembering that, in the Westminster words, "The purest churches under heaven are subject to both mixture and error." We must not dare to assume to know what God has withheld. Logic is pallid beside the changing emphasis of life. Scholarship is only genuine when it keeps itself synonymous with discipleship. Statement advances under the tuition of God and demands restatement.

> "The fathers had not all of Thee;
> New births are in thy grace;
> All open to our souls shall be
> Thy Spirit's hiding place."

"Take heed lest there shall be any one that maketh spoil of you thro his philosophy and vain deceit, after the rudiments of the world, and not after Christ."

So said the apostle, (Col. 2:8), who boldly wrote, "We know in part,"—imperfectly.

No chemical formula can state what a child is to his mother. As soon as we redistribute truth, we have missed an inherent somewhat, that eludes analysis. °We must not identify mannikin with man. The vital secret evades the clinic. The law of life refuses an equation.

Analysis is like turning a stocking inside out to mend it; synthesis is like turning it back to wear it. But it is not quite the same. When we divide and recombine, the result carries the marks of the process; a certain original naturalness necessarily has escaped. One can never unpack and perfectly repack an egg. He can perhaps restore the matter but not the arrangement. It can be eaten but it will not hatch. Bees do not hover over artificial flowers. Partially, (of course!) all this can suggest that while wisdom furnished the outfit of a propositional theology, that wisdom was revealed in a more excellent way. The permission to philosophize is also the inculcation of humility. In the word, as in the world, suggestion is shoreless; truth is fluid, not frozen—molten, not molded. Here is a man, not anatomy; here are wells, not cisterns; tides, not ripples; a sky full—fathomlessly full—of stars, not a stellar map, which is a tabled surface without depths and backgrounds.

Botany has its merits, but its herbarium is not a garden. We want it, but we want more the perfume of revelation, rooted and growing. Our laboratories can never supersede the chemistry of May. Creation is a poem, translatable (partly) into prose, but appealing to feeling as prose cannot. God is a poet and man is His epic. Euclid and Aristotle furnish one much, but John Zebedee, and Paul, offer more.

Even heroic bronze and marble borrow from the beholder. Their metonomy is only vindicated in his memory. Any theodicy that is not punctuated with interrogation marks requires that the proof-reader shall insert exclamations.

Our catenas may include more or less of the priceless attar, but they are all brittle vessels and some to honor and some to dishonor. No single period has exhausted God or man. There are always surds. Whatever is alive is mobile. Any theory that announces its completeness digs its own grave.

Identity, with its personal relations, continues, but our bodies die daily. The man never outgrows his father, while he puts away many childish things — clothes and their fashions, notions and their phrases, and so at last he attains true childlikeness and "finds the blessedness of being little." And theology, unless it has exchanged plasticity for ossification, retires from its volumes this and that conjectural and tenuous paragraph and rewrites its translation with pain and purging. To say "there can be nothing new in theology," is either to dismiss its assistance, or to make of it a graven image and imitate the stagnant decrees of the Council of Trent. It is to say, "I have found out the Almighty to perfection," and is as impious as it would be to say "there can be nothing new in astronomy!" Each better telescope has that boast in derision. No, the glory of this cathedral is that it is unfinished. The soundest theology knows that it is the quotient, or rather the multiple of truth and experience. The *obiter dicta* of men too often deny the authenticity of inspiration and lead toward Deism. When we go with the Living God, we change our maps. It is true of Him, but never of us — "there is no parallax, nor eclipse."

By no post-mortem, of the third century or of the sixteenth, are we to find what man is to believe concerning God, or what duties God requires of man; but by heeding the ever-consistent and ever-persistent Spirit of Christ. Faith cannot be copied or copyrighted. As we come out of the damp and indoor air of man-made explanations, our lungs and eyes both do better. Having sat at the feet of Gamaliel, we fall on our faces before the noon-transcendent Christ and re-learn.

It is just so far as opinion corrects itself by His word, as "the only infallible rule," that it has any claim to speak or be heard. The "unadultered milk," is "the simplicity that is in Christ." We should be grateful to all serious and modest souls who have handled the problems of divinity, and we must "imitate their faith," by handling these for ourselves. Their warrant is ours, too. They acknowledged no mortmain and we cannot. No syllabus is an ultimatum; it is rather like the catalog of a living library, accurate to date. It may be a good index, but never can exhaust all the cross-references.

That catholic man and tireless student, Henry B. Smith, said well: "He who asserts that there is no truth in past systems and thinks to make one wholly original, and he who asserts that the whole of truth, in its most perfect form, is given us in the formulas of the past, and only there, each of them is equally distant from the just equilibrium. \* \* The whole history of theology gives but the attempt to reproduce the contents of scripture in the forms needed by the different times in which the different systems were made."

Those weighty syllables contain what I mean, that the church militant is a church marching, that as the sun rises the shadows shift and shorten, that all ongoing swings the horizon. No two battles are the same, even if issued upon the same field. Certain defences are abandoned when the enemy attacks flank or rear. Silenced batteries and spiked guns are worth no further powder. Change of strategy is not surrender. They used to complain of Bonaparte that he violated the accustomed evolutions of battle. It was that supreme genius in tactics who said "the army that stays in its entrenchments beaten." Surely one is not disloyal to the constitution of these United States, because heartily approving its amendments. Our bright flag is not the same that waved first on land at Fort Stanwix, then at Trenton, upon Lake Erie and over Fort Sumter: but we love it because it expresses growth in its revision. We keep the stripes and make room for all the stars that come. Franklin and Adams, Hamilton and Madison and Marshall were sturdy patriots: but they were not the last of the line.

Well then, at last I approach my main contention and I would express my conviction of the proper distinction between theology and creed. It is one of uses. A creed should express attitude as well as opinion, and it must be portable. Creeds are guidons and banners. They are symbols and standards. They should be emblems not encyclopedias — titles rather than indexes. The best are those that are the most vivid and pity, writ in large letters and short words. A good creed affirms facts not inferences. The Te Deum which I would call the best confession of faith since that of the Apostle Thomas, is not abstract nor is it panoramic. Moreover it is lyrical. The best creed will be adoring rather than explanatory. It will be positive and personal and will prompt, and perhaps supply, anthems. Ascription is a higher and more influential tribute than subscription. Creeds are the landmarks of great campaigns. They have always punctuated the progress of the church. The elaborate amplifications of Augsburg, Dort, and the rest showed the competency of the reformation to antagonize its terrible foes. I admire the massive masonry and revere it services; these are bastions; but while I am impressed, I am not attracted. "I cannot go with these for I have not proved them."

The regulative principle of these great symbols, is the nonfinality of all human statements. In their bold affirmativeness and determined revision they emphasize a progress to which they could and would set no period.

That venerable chapter will not be erased. It is exemplary. What they saw they said.

Holmes says "Seience is the art of packing knowledge." The folios and quartos should be kept accessible: but they do not forbid the handier duodecimo. There can be little doubt that the New England primer has done more educating than Turretin. There is nothing holy about a polysyllable. I plead for shorter statements not shallower, for clearness not weakness, for a closer front, for increased distinctness. The church is the servant and trustee of a definite gospel. She knows whom she has believed, and is bound both to confess Christ before men, and evermore to ask —"what think ye of HIM?"

Christianity is a life based upon commitment to Christ as the Saviour from sin. This is the calyx and cover. Let us stand at this centre and so have word, work, and worship all concentric and all Christian, not incidentally but elementally. Providence is the radius swung about that point! Assuredly that will be most Patro-centric which is most Christo-centric. To the credulity of infidelity, to the dogmatic agnosticism which denies the knowledge of God, to the bigotry of indifference, and to the sharp-set creed of creedlessness, we are confidently and constantly to affirm the love of God in Christ as the law of life.

That "liberalism" which would resolve the church into a debating society and change the thesis of the cross into hypothesis chooses to renounce the sweep and summons of the Christian facts.

That is slovenly thinking that wants to read time by a "liberal" chronometer, weigh duty in a "liberal" scales, and steer by a "liberal" compass. We do not want less fibre, but more. We would not abandon our positions, but defend them with modern ordnance. We would have statements that in all their length and breadth can stand not only the dialectical test, but what is far more searching, the homiletical test.

There is a cheap and glib assault upon the Westminster confession by those who have not read it, and to whom serious and careful thought is so irksome, that they would not appreciate it if they had. Here is a declaration and testimony whose influence witnesses the learning and wisdom of its sponsors. It was the precipitate of a great age. It has vigor and sap. It is vertebrated and erect. It was written between prayers. It gave a sheet-anchor to England and Scotland, too, when church and state were all adrift. It has stood so long and served so well because it was so good and such an advance upon its predecessors. It has been so conservative because it was so positive. It is strong because it denies so much error, and explains so much truth.

I would neither undervalue nor overvalue it. "We know in part." It cannot be that the last statement under that momentous verb *credo* (in which man should be at once at his loftiest and his lowliest) was written in 1649 ! I can assent *bona fide* and *con amore* to that instrument as containing a system of doctrine warranted by the Scripture. I cannot say that it is the system Scripture teaches; for Scripture does not teach by system nor can I say that it is the only system Scripture warrants; for that would be to denounce the point of view of other Christian brethren who by their fruits may be known to be as near to God as we are, and yet who have built their philosophical house another way. I like it far better than any other system man has so far made; but it is a little long for a creed. Systems will do as garrison flags — 36 feet long; creeds are better at the regimental measure of 6 feet and 6 inches.

I would therefore see a new statement to avoid both the deficiencies and the redundancies of this. My feeling is that many of its inferences are extra-Biblical and some infra-Biblical. It does not do equal justice to the different summits in God's range of attributes. But I do not desire to criticise this house that has sheltered so many of my ancestors. I do not want to see it tinkered, mangled, desecrated, changed from its identity into some dichromatic eccentricity which would have the faults of two periods with the strength of neither.

I make no apology for referring to the attempt and failure of four years ago. That movement toward a so-called revision failed for many reasons and with few to mourn, When the committee said to the presbyteries, "how will this do?" the more part replied, "it will not do."

There were some who wanted nothing changed and who were satisfied that the Confession was good for 250 years longer.

There were some who wanted numerous verbal changes and some paragraphs modified, but who liked the philosophical method and held to its permanent adequacy.

And there were some who thought that all revision would be either too much or too little; who thought a brief, ardent and profoundly evangelical statement could well be made now for actual uses in our churches, not one in twenty of whose members know practically anything of the Westminster confession. A true creed should be popular rather than official. It should be both handy and hearty.

Of those who then urged the need of such a creed I am thankful to say I was one, and I have ventured to broach this subject now, because I firmly believe the recent postponements have but increased the demand and the duty.

It should be written in full recognitiou of the value of past creeds and of their necessary temporariness. It should not attempt to sketch the whole coast line of present Christian knowledge; bui should present all the great lighthouse headlands. It should be warm, thankful, and martial, a "confession of hope" too, one that could be joyfully used and clearly understood in Christian worship, and that would furnish an entirely adequate test of official loyalty to the everlasting gospel and the ever-crescent kingdom of God's dear Son. The seventeenth century wrote its noble chapter and said what it honestly believed. It was definitive then. For its time it was generous and conciliatory. Why should not we do as much for our day? Why should we imitate Pharoah's command to the midwives and if the cry is that of a man-child, kill it? Even Canute set down his own foot as a mark for the sea. True reverence is not afraid and does not face two ways. It thanks God for the wonderfully augmented apparatus and for the intense, sanctified study of two centuries. Only bourbonism in religion thinks that God's clocks were all stopped at the time of the Long Parliament. Even Rome has new popes. Declaring them infallible, she has not yet decreed them non-mortal! The pillar of flame is still vanguard and rereward of the church, and only anchylosis—stiffening of the joints—refuses to march.

That stormy Westminster assembly did its noble best, and the liberty of the gospel—"strenous liberty," permits and invites us to a blessing we greatly need, that of actually telling what we actually hold, and flinging a flag to all the winds of heaven, without ambiguity and without anachronism. I say with Baxter, "Do not make more necessary articles than God hath done. Let no man's writings or the judgment of any party be made that test." I refer to the wise words of Calvin (in the fourth book of his Institutes) concerning church councils. "When the voice of God (one has well said) ceases to speak, silence becomes the only orthodoxy. "Credo" is to be said in the present tense, not the imperfect, nor the future-perfect; in the indicative mood, not in the subjunctive or imperative! I do not plead for the apocopation of statement; but on the contrary for one so clear that it shall tempt no one toward demoralizing sophistication and sublimation. I believe there never was an age better fitted to write its creed. But fit or not, and under the scornful challenges to our sincerity, it is pusillanimous not to be willing to try. A period that is unwilling to write its real creed is unworthy to say any! Brief, but not bare; ample, but not prolix; neither indefinite nor drastic; not pointing like a rusted vane to the windward of yesterday; playing neither at Procrustes nor at Tantatus; neither withdrawing the offense of the cross, nor offering fully to solve all its universal meanings—such a creed the world would welcome and respect. It could mightily bless the Presbyterian Church to write its manifesto of what it was prepared to live for and die for! We must not expect more of a creed than it can do. It cannot excuse us from hard thinking, nor from hard work in carrying it out to the proof of life. I hail the movement to state the actual present faith of the church as the sign that the Omnipresent and Supreme Spirit is leading toward other Pentecosts. Mental growing pains are the proof of His contact. The Rock will stand. It is not in jeopardy. Neither violent foes nor timid friends can shake it. God will teach us His own accent if we will ask His approval only and utter all that He gives. This alert, sensitive, confused, and yet earnest and plastic age so greatly needs the true meaning of the genuine Church of Christ, that I long to see all ecclesiastical impedimenta sent to the rear.

The plain issue is so mortal and so painful that we can well afford to let the ecclesiast and the logician pass by so that the humane Son of God can lift and bear and heal. A shorter statement and a longer arm say I, for one.

Now, "He standeth behind our wall. He looketh in at the windows. He showeth Himself thro the lattice."

Yet a little while and "we shall know, even as also we have been known," Him "in whom are hid all the treasures both of the wisdom and knowledge of God," who said "I am come that ye might have life and more abundantly;" Him, "of the increase of whose government there shall be no end."

  Thou Holy, Omnipresent One,
   Of God's whole Church the only Guide!
  Thy gifts, at Pentecost begun,
   Thro every age are multiplied.

  Above the heads of fervent men
   Still burns the unconsuming flame,
  And Thou dost utterance give again
   To speak with tongues in Jesus' name.

  In every land and language, Thou
   One mighty work dost still increase,
  Perplexing earthly wisdom now,—
   For Babel discords giving peace.

  Man's spirit is Thy lamp, O Light!
   Wherewith to search the inmost part.
  Obedience shall not walk in night,
   Nor guiding fail the craving heart.

  Thy Scripture speaketh not in vain
   Of all the yearning love Thou hast
  That man should in Thy life attain
   That sky no doubt can overcast!

## EXPECTANT ATTENTION

We trust Thee, God, forever near!
  Not timid lest Thou be withdrawn;
Each century makes Thy word more clear,
  And shall, till day eternal dawn.

We dare not heed another hand,
  Nor hark to any lesser voice,
Give Thou Thy truth to understand,
  And make that truth our only choice!

# Partisanship and Patriotism

*A RESPONSE AT THE "HARDWARE DINNER"*
*HOTEL SAVOY, NEW YORK CITY*
*FEBRUARY 20, 1896*

*Mr. President and Fellow-citizens:*

It was a remark which I have seen attributed to Sydney Smith, upon his leave-taking with a departing missionary, "Sir, I hope you will agree with the man that eats you"! It always struck me that the indigestibility of Jonah must have been instructive to that fish whose hospitality was so unsuccessful and so brief. Both the monster and the medicine must have had wiser notions as to quick sails and small prophets.

A little while ago I talked behind a table in this city and did not finish until the next day! The presiding officer intimated that I was the last man who should speak that night, and he was right. I began by congratulating those who had already left and then asked leave to print. I would say to my fellow morsels who are appetizingly displayed at this counter, that I know what it is to hold my thumbs and wonder if there is to be any time left. I am credibly informed that the Holland Society is responsible for first running a dinner with a windmill. The fluidity of the Dutch Republic may have much to do with the fluency of which we are now in the habit at several dollars a plate. Men used to take naps as an aid to digestion, now they hear speeches. Let us make the most of it while it lasts. The next thing will be something else. The peerless lay-preacher who in his less occupied moments presides over the only four track road in America is one of the chief sponsors for this decade of ventriloquism. All of us can admire where none can emulate his scintillating facility. Not pretending to offer you anything so stimulating in its effervescence, I would try to persuade you that Apollinaris is as good and even better if you only think so! I am a preacher and a college professor. There are some who are ready to assume that preaching and teaching make a man an impracticable, a spinner of theories without real relation to average and actual affairs. If there are those here who think that preaching is, in Mr. Huxley's polite phrase, "lunar politics," and that a college is a school of cranks, I will not challenge them nor argue the point. I am a man. I am an American. I am a citizen. I trust that I am a Christian. These grounds are solid leverage for my present purpose. From them I speak. And from these I say that he is no true minister who is not evermore busy to show how all desirable good rests in the recognition of ultimate principles, and who is not urgent to compel all matters of custom and practice to testify before the grand jury of conscience. And I say again that any College abuses its opportunity if it does not seek to inspire its every student with ideals which are most practical when they are most generous, and to base him broad and strong with the conviction that his better training is a holy trust for larger manhood and for the most resolute, intelligent and robust citizenship. It is the human duty of us all, whatever our antecedents, our attainment, or our occupations, to help make this a larger and pleasanter world for every man that is in it. We can only do this as our love steadily becomes more dominant, and as we more and more widen our comprehension of that high relationship in which all men are kin. Not the word "My," but "Our," begins the Lord's Prayer. The man who prays:

"Lord, bless me and my wife,
My son John and his wife,
Us four and no more, Amen,"—

that man does not pray at all, and, preaching tho it may be, I say that a man who does not pray does not live! In this state which holds the ashes of John Brown, in this city, which keeps the dust of Alexander Hamilton and of Ulysses Grant, you are assembled in the name of a common business interest. This dining emphasizes a commonalty, a community, a cooperativeness of purpose. It is what men have in common, not what they have in severalty, that fulfils their life. That which unites men is normal, that which sunders them is abnormal. It is not because we are states, but because we are United States, that we are a nation. But real union can not be an external device, it must be an inward truth.

In my eagerness to affirm a great principle, as wide as all life, and comprehensive of all human relation, I am aware of a peril of becoming too abstract. An aged woman in Alabama was with her husband, taking her first ride on the cars. Her wonder and anxiety increased with the speed, until at the top of her astonishment and fear, the train struck a long and high trestle. With a scream the woman bounded to her feet, clutching the seat-back before her. To her trembling obliviousness of all else it seemed that the cars had leaped into space. But in a brief moment the train was on terra firma once more, and with a happy shout heard thro all the car, she cried: "Thank Heaven, she's lit again!" Gentlemen, if for a little here and there, I seem to you to be in the air, I assure all who have tickets for this trip that I shall try not to leave the rails!

What is partisanship? It is identification with a part. A party is a section — bipartisanship is bisection. To see no more than a part is to ignore the whole. A part is a part only. The sum of parts is the true goal. A part divorced from its fellow parts is a part no longer. Your arm wrenched from its body is not your arm! Parts and parties are means, partnership is the end. The word idiot is from a Greek adjective meaning selfish. It is an introspection which becomes mental blindness. Individuality, by exageration, becomes insanity. The vice of selfishness is in its isolation from a common life. Its secession is centrifugal — the atom resenting the universal law of unity. In the heart it is hate, in the life it is war, in essence it is hell. The bane of partisanship in whatever realm and to whatever scale is in its arbitrary exclusion of relation. Give and take,— mutuality, reciprocity,— is the law of a balanced life. A year ago Senator John Sherman rose in his place to insist that "measures for the relief of the treasury should be viewed from a higher standpoint than partisanship," and he said: "If I were to think of party or party advantage in proposing legislation to protect the government credit, I would be guilty of violating my oath of office." Yes and Amen. But if that be true, where does it not reach? Well may we, in such days as these, pray in the words of the Psalm, that God would "teach our senators wisdom" of that sort! In Congress or out of it, he is false to his country who is a partisan first and a patriot afterward. Each of us is guilty of a treasonable narrowness who prefers tactics to truth. It is ungenerous and degrading to refuse to recognize the excellences and persistently to impugn the good faith of those who differ from us in their philosophy. The bonds of civil life and of national loyalty are strained and broken when we vituperate our magistrates merely because they did not happen to have the preference of our particular votes. Whoever the President of my country is, he is the President of my country! Two things debauch our politics—one is money, the other acrimony. We are all of us too much Tillmanized. The man who thinks to exalt himself merely by depreciating others and who glories in his hostilities rather than his friendships, but exhibits his own semi-civilized estate.

So long and so far as we consent to send mere party mercenaries and not statesmen, to make our laws, so long and so far will bitterness and sectional advantage override considerations of that weal which ought always to precede the prestige of a faction. We are all to much the constituents of a false theory, and we pay the penalties. A little tyrant, three years old, was kicking and screaming at his nurse. It was on the cars, and the passengers all longed to spank the small autocrat. He wanted a wasp that crept on the window sill. He tried to take it. The nurse caught his hand and said coaxingly: "Harry mustn't touch. Bug bite Harry." Harry screamed savagely and began to kick and pound the nurse. The dozing mother, without opening her eyes or lifting her head, said sharply: "Why do you tease that child so, Mary? Let him have what he wants at once." "But ma'am, it's a—" "Let him have it, I say." Thus encouraged Harry clutched at the wasp and caught it. The scream that followed brought tears of joy to the passengers' eyes. The mother roused again. "Mary," she cried, "let him have it." Mary turned in her seat and said, confusedly: "He's got it, ma'am."

> "When we in our viciousness grow hard,
> The wise gods seal our eyes. * * *
> In our own filth drop our clear judgments; make us
> Adore our errors; laugh at us, while we strut
> To our confusion."

The braggart spirit anywhere is absurd. Some little school girls (it is chronicled of Chicago) were discussing their clothes. "I've a lovely new dress," said one, "and I'm going to wear it to church next Sunday." "Pooh!" said another, "I've a new hat, and I'm going to wear it every day." "Well," said a third, "I've got heart disease, anyway!" The two were mute with envy. She was a Populist! Must minorities always be truculent and majorities always be insolent? Yes, while party is put above principle: No, when that infamy ends. Unless one is willing to be a mere political fashionist whose german-silver principles, like those of Bunyan's By-Ends, are 'at once harmless and profitable,' he may not prefer clique to character, and a mean success to an honorable defeat. He must not confuse pro party and *pro patria*, nor bow and cross himself at the beck of a civil ultra-montanism that would mother devotion by ignorance; but must protest, tho he be but one *contra mundum*, and vote as it were a sacrament. Better 'vote in the air' than vote in the mud! When the air is full it will snow victory. To heed that brazen and bitter cry: "Party, right or wrong," disgraces the soul and sears the vision. Nothing is more immoral, more ruinous of personal honor, than to succumb to that social coercion of the 'straight ticket,' which has lost most of its terrors for men whose spines are not bits of wet string—mere boneless marrow, but which has so long ostracized independence, and in the name of Cæsar usurped the things of God. Softening of the back may be as fatal as softening of the brain. I am thankful to live in a commonwealth whose vote party bell-wethers so often fail to predict by a hundred thousand majority. Electoral unindependence is political serfdom. The discriminating voter is evidently in the right way because he so bothers and exasperates bad men.

"When none will sweat but for promotion;" when demagogs "make nice of no vile hold to stay them up;" when legislators are often so notorious that self-respect must pray— "unto their assembly mine honor be not thou united;" when "the most upright is as a thorn hedge" (combing wool from every passing sheep) taking toll both ways; when the indirect but debauching bribe of patronage would make office but a carcass for the swiftest vulture; when Truth is about to be recrucified between bipartisans, no decent man can wash his hands with Pilate and say "I am innocent, see ye to it!"

Of course statesmen, like Demetrius, the silversmith, seeing the craft by which they have their wealth in danger to be set at naught, will raise the specious cry "Great is Diana"—always, "of the Ephesians."

Of course honest citizenship will be resisted, claw and tooth, by those "whose mouths (as Lowell said) are filled with the national pudding, or watering in expectation thereof." All the more must it withstand and smite that lust of spoils which would wreck the stateliest cause to make flotsam and jetsam of every public trust from president to poundmaster. The belly of the great machine "teems with armed men!" Left alone within the walls, they will after dark do all their fell intent. In our own Troy, that revolver at the polls, finding its victim, was a danger signal that only deaf souls can forget. 'Party, at any price,' is that which prostitutes republican institutions, and with the malaria of its ill breath poisons us all.

It exhales pestilence and breeds corruption.

Must it ever be the task of Sisyphus to rescue the primary from that exploitation by hucksters which makes the individual citizen but a blank proxy? Shall platforms always be mere verbal expedients — gull-baits, — declarations of proposals that are not purposes, of crafty phrases without intent, and whose quotation after the polls close is considered to be a roaring farce? Are we always to be fed on platitudes? Is the originating force of those costly campaigns, which ought always to advance the lines of loyal purpose, to lodge in the councils of honest and earnest citizens fairly and freely assembled, or in the back office of self appointed and power-stealing autocrats who with ambi-sinister facility slit the throats of cities, impose tribute upon firms and corporations, or amuse goggle-eyed credulity while twitching the wires that work respectable and unsuspecting men as marionettes?

Is the selection of candidates to be relegated to the stage management of these Punch-and-Judy showmen?

When the primary and the caucus and the convention are cajoled, intimidated, packed, perverted, they cease to become representative, and only rivet the shackles upon those who in their surrender to an insolent arrogation of proprietorship reduce themselves to servility and moral impotence. It is an impudence that makes the average voter a puppet. Dr. Jekyll becomes Mr. Hyde. The voice is Trilby's, but the song is Svengali's! The auction of the voter is completed in "the sale of law." Moral inertia, lotus-eating indifference, crass selfishness, a materialistic and mercantile theory of life;— these things "tend downwards, justify despondency, promote rogues, defeat the lust," and will, just so long as voters consent to be shovelled, or to be done up in express packages to be delivered C. O. D., at owner's risk! Poor Sinbad! Whoever those possible nominees of 1896 may be whom these steerers and confidence men least want, them the respectable part of this company most is for!

How the municipality problem lours with portent, in all its

subordinate details of drunkenness, lechery, bribery, simony and sleek coupon-cutting apathy. Kill me that last and I will render you the heads of all the rest! When shall we adequately resist the intolerant imposture and intolerable duress of underlings and send truly representative men to the councils of the nation? Think of a state that owned a George William Curtis, that contains a St. Clair McKelway and an Elihu Root, persistently preferring some of the second-rate partisans who have strutted into the United States Senate! I would that I could make these words strike and detonate like percussion shells! We need unconditional men, indomitable souls, who shall, to all that would wheedle or coerce them, utter a rigid—'No! Patriotism first, Party afterward.' We are grateful for the noble few who are such as ennoble their constituents in refusing the pettings of ringleaders and the trammels of mediocrity, and in living toward their parties that fine sentiment which the cavalier of Lovelace utters to his Lucasta,—

"I could not love thee, dear, so much
Loved I not honor more."

Never did a time more need noble leadership. Must we always flout our living prophets, and ever be lamenting a dead Lincoln? Must the witchcraft of foul selfishness always stupefy and strangle us with its incantations? Worthy thought will be incarnate in worthy men when we summon such. As yet we do not seek them. We consent to partisan dishonor. "Democracy can be justified only in so far as it furnishes the most effective method of securing wise and just rulers: but in a democracy this end can only be attained in so far as every citizen fulfils his civic obligations." All peoples have as good a government and as good governors as they demand, no better. All improvement begins in new convictions. The best things are offered only to the best men. Our theory confronts us with our condition. At present sectionalism and class legislation hold us up at every turn, and localism laughs at the general good. We think that law can repeal arithmetic. A great mob of inflationists clamors for more money. By an artifice it would set a fictitious value upon silver and ask the world to believe that 50 cents is 100. At that rate all the silver of the Earth would come in here "by telegram at our expense." Why not declare that a bushel of wheat is a dollar, that a barrel of oil is two dollars, build elevators and tanks, take the whole product, and offer warehouse certificates for these stores as money at this fanciful rate? Money has either an intrinsic value or an extrinsic. These are not to be confused. If the present light-weight dollar, with its counterfeit of Liberty and its hypocritical profession of faith (for a false balance is an abomination, and sanctimony is poor currency)—if such a dollar, of which the Treasury has 300,000,000 that no one wants at the price asked,—if such a dollar's value is extrinsic, 16 to 1 is too much, by 16; if intrinsic it is too little by 13. If we as sellers at that rate, would try to foist an anachronism upon the world, it won't buy: if we are buyers at that rate it will joyfully accommodate us with its last ounce.

Remember, Gentlemen, that those who are so eager to double the coinage value of silver over the actual bullion value, are those who have silver to sell! In comparison with those who listen to the invitations of these silver sirens, Aladdin's wife was astute! Why not coin copper free at sixteen to one, and so 'boom' an American product? Such a chimera would indeed make us all money-maniacs and America a veritable *asylum* of all nations! It would be no less "woolly" to assert that eighteen inches is a yard. England would gladly sell to us at such a rate, she would not buy. The whole thing illustrates the great truth that 'every man has his price'—*who is for sale?* I do not object to a metal—I object to a ratio that is a lie. "Sixteen to one," is obsolete. To have two values for a dollar is a fatuity over which I feel like the preacher who, standing in the pulpit of a son who had gone daft over ecclesiastical millinery, took for his text—"Lord, have mercy upon my son, for he is a lunatic!" Inflation is balloonacy. A nation which in two supreme crises so grandly determined to be free, shall never blandly consent to be dishonest; which in such a seven-heated furnace learned the sixth commandment and the seventh, shall not repudiate the fourth at the bidding of rum, nor the eighth at the bidding of silver mines. At last the tenth shall round into the first, and "Thou shalt not covet" shall touch "Thou shalt have no other God." Happy is the people that is in such a case! How far class envy can go is shown in the artificial provisions of that preposterous inter-state commerce act which at present is prostrating the greatest industry of the land, flinging scores of roads into the hands of receivers and robbing the incomes of numberless employes, and of widows and orphans whose savings it slaughters. Its provisions are mainly based upon an envious particularism which is both sumptuary and socialistic.

But I forget that I am only a country parson, and I preach too long. You noticed yesterday that the 'Cave of the Winds' had gone dry! I will speak of Patriotism. Pater means father, the Patria is the fatherland. Patriotism is brotherhood, and it has no limits. As a family that seeks only its own advantage is a curse to its community, so too, a nation that seeks only its own good is a curse to the world, and ultimately to itself. Shall there ever be a truly Christian nation? Does liberty only mean "*our* liberty?" If the ethics of the gospel are not fit to be national, they are not fit to be personal. But how many nations have learned the ten commandments, let alone the beatitudes? Patriotism is but a geographical partisanship if its ultimate notions are unfraternal to mankind. Too many in their handling of that word illustrate what the recent Century has described as "the effect of a large idea upon a small mind." "Make me pure (prayed a little girl) make me as pure as baking powder!" We have lately been discussing the merits of Royal baking powder and Cleveland's. But the question of which of these contains the least alum and the most force is not so important as that we should seek to have all the world join us at the knees of God in that petition: "Give us this day our daily bread!" Partisanship is sectional, patriotism is national; nay, it is international. Whatever may be my secondary and subordinate relations, primarily I am a man. Anything less than loyalty to the whole cause of mankind is secession from God.

> "The peoples, Lord, the peoples,
> Not thrones and crowns, but men."

"Have we not all one father?" As patriotism is above party, so is humanity above diplomacy. "Let not thy country (said fine old Sir Thomas Browne) — let not the law of thy country be the non-ultra of thine honesty." What are the questions of Venezuela and the Suez canal, what is even the harsh question of Cuba, by the side of the world disgrace over Armenia!

Thank God the American protest has been made. Shame to England that her tumescent Lord Salisbury passes by on the other side. Shame to all alleged Christian nations that there is not a new crusade to abolish that hideous and piratical power whose cimetar is the corrollary of its Koran. Oh, for another Cromwell, Peter the Hermit, Charles Martel, to smite utterly this cruel absolutism. Oh, for another Coeur de Lion. What is an empty sepulchre whence the Lord of life is risen to the perishing myriads for whom he came! God of armies, bare Thy holy arm against that livid, curdled and putrescent misgovernment that sets its crescent above the city of Constantine, and seduces nations to forget that watchword of the cross, *In Hoc signo vinces!* How can any sneer at the brave words from Washington that invite a new holy alliance against that malign despotism. There might be a thanksgiving dinner of the world if Russia and England would cease their flatulent haggling over the wishbone! Would that the bleeding 'Eastern questions' were delivered not only out of the hand of the uncircumcised Philistine, but also out of the paw of the Lion and of the Bear!

I for one am grateful for that pertinent apothegm of the Brooklyn *Eagle* — it was indeed eagle-eyed — "What is fundamentally right is also profoundly wise!" Oh, the cowardice of the ledger and the bank book--"letting I dare not, wait upon, I would!" It refills a religious cult, emptied of Christianity, with that old exclusive provincialism which slew Christ, and makes his house of prayer for all nations into a stock exchange!

Gentlemen, America is providential. She is adapted to be an almoner and an arbiter of nations. Let us interpret destiny by duty, honor by service, opportunity by responsibility, and so

"Set up a mark of everlasting light
Above the howling senses ebb and flow,"

that we shall enter into the task and so alone into the triumph of the Son of Man! For *vox recti populi, vox Dei!*

Let us lift the non-partisan, the truly patriotic standard both of national righteousness and of a world-wide sympathy, of the true partnership of man under the one paternity of God. Let Rome stand for force and statute, Greece for culture, Germany for learning, France for art, England for diplomacy and aggrandizement, all these for war; and we, in God's name, for character, for inter-national and super-political justice, for real freedom, and for the ever-nearer dominion of the Prince of Peace.

Domain, ancestry, heritage, however much — we are not merely to follow, but to fulfill our fathers, "God having provided some better thing for us, that they without us should not be made perfect."

Here lies the nobility of both men and of nations. Here is truth that has no barrier of river or mountain, no bound of sea or shore. All of us for America and for all America, and America for all mankind!

# The Distinctive Function of the College

### REMARKS BEFORE THE UNIVERSITY CLUB
### OF BUFFALO, NEW YORK
### MARCH 3, 1896

*Gentlemen of the University Club:* You are not associated under this title by caprice or mere casual impulse. You began and you continue this fellowship for the sufficient reason that you have certain important common interests which by organization you desire to proclaim and to promote.

You affirm, as do similar bodies in now so many of our major cities, the accordant aims and the substantial good will of all men liberally educated. You also affirm your joint relation to the public good.

Your two hundred and fifty members, in representation of fifty colleges, is no meagre showing, and it is a high credit, as it ought also to become a broad benefit, to the city which is the third in our preeminent state, and in the nation the eleventh.

Each of us here loves well his own academic cradle, and is a perpetual debtor to the hand that rocked it. Each of us cherishes the songs of his own college fireside. But we are all of kin and bear a family likeness. The several *Almæ Matres* to whom we owe our baccalaureate birthrights are one large and loving sisterhood and we are warm first cousins. We are the alumni (or nurslings) of one grandmother, and her name is Σοφία. While the timbers stand that uphold the great ancestral and homestead roof of American education, may Wisdom be justified of her children! The tie which is expressed by such a sodality or guild as this, both confesses and strengthens a partnership of competency, of aspiration, and of purpose.

The relatively large ratio of influence so far exerted in our land by its College men is a commanding fact, too often neglected. To us it should be full not of vapid self-praise but of ardent stimulations. It is a commission, and it lays upon every true-souled College man a thrilling *noblesse oblige*. It is a badge that is morally a pledge,— a pledge that we alone can vindicate and that we alone can smirch and degrade. This throng is a part of that providential endowment of skilled and equipped manhood which should and shall have great share in meeting the inevitable and impending battles of the age, and, in Truth's name, in turning them into victories beyond precedent or imagination. The beneficiaries of singular privilege, we are bound to be the exponents of singular power. The benefit we partake is ours not to hoard or squander but to transmit. We are bound not only to resent but to refute the little sneers that impugn scholarship as tending toward either the impractical or the unsympathetic. Our banners many but our flag one, without selfishness or schism let all our varied colors blend in one prismatic white. Echoing the spirit of that gallant greeting of England's poet,—

> "Come to us, love us, and make us your own,
> For Saxon or Dane or Norman we,
> Teuton or Celt, or whatever we be,
> We are each all Dane in our welcome of thee,
>   Alexandra! —

so be our loyal acclaim to the princess *Duty*.

I said, *Noblesse oblige*. That may be the mere boast of titular precedence, of hereditary assumption. But where the nobility is essential, moral, genuine, not the freak and accident of birth; where it stands for character not class, it is not a duress but a consecration. The real "war-lord" never poses nor struts. He is a captain because not bellicose, and imperial because not imperious — chief because the servant of all. With no European, but with a royally American accent, in the aristocracy of democracy, true nobility affirms itself not in a clannish condescension but in a humane and therefore manly social creed. So meant, it binds all better ability to quit a cloistered intellectual luxury, and to give itself to better the world. So meant, its claim is verified in the generosity of unstinted helps. For just as agriculture is not for the field's sake, but for the harvest's, so mental culture is for human use and social result. More strength, more strain. More mind, more man.

It is by recognizing such ends, and by combining toward them the abilities and impulses otherwise scattered, and so less efficient, that clubs like this are to warrant their name and propriety. Your social pleasure, if it is to be worthy, must move toward the moral alliance and augment of personal convictions concerning the questions of this decade of the passing century, with its huge pride and need, its dangers and its susceptibilities. Organization, as an end, is mere addition—as a means toward ends that lie beyond individual strengths, it is multiplication. Surely there are problems enough, civic and national, moral and mental, to make royal demands upon all taught and trained citizens, and to constrain such to draw together and to stand together. A really educated manliness is sacred to service and sworn to the general good, and the ethical compulsions of such an election and calling are as beautiful to willing souls as they are austere toward the reluctant and the recluse. The high summons that implies high tasks carries in its left hand to those who reject such a summons the stern penalty of missing these tasks.

You, gentlemen, are distinctively and representatively *College men*. "University" is to be sure more comprehensive: but in this connection it is metonomy. Not as Masters of Arts, or of Science,—not as Doctors of Philosophy, Divinity, Literature, or Laws: but as Batchelors are you here bound and blended. The A. B. degree is your common ground. Those distinguish, this unites. Whatever else you have, you are here because you have this. Its relation to the rest is basilar. It still carries with it the most of *prima facie* proof. Less than any other title has it been tarnished and deteriorated and cheapened by brevet use. The chevron often certifies more than does the epaulet. Let the A. B. be reserved from miscellaneous bestowal. To use a little Latin, let us say the *nunc pro tunc* should be a *quid pro quo*, and should be given only for the stiff four years which it crowns, or for their most genuine equivalent.

To a company, then, of those who primarily are Batchelors of Arts, and whose coordination founds upon that fact, I make the theme of these remarks (which are stipulated to be but conversational)—*The distinctive function of the College, as such.* I shall not be misunderstood to seek an adroit obtruding of my own environment, nor to be doing any indirect advertising, when I speak from the view point which that environment has furnished me. If at some tangents I shall challenge some of the views here held, you must permit me to be frank rather than diplomatic. These opinions are not polemical, nor are they deprecatory. You will I am sure allow me an area of the freest speech.

The College is a distinct and indigenous thing in American education, with firm and clear limitations. It has history—deep roots, wide branches, fair and abundant fruitage. It stands between Academy and University and is neither. It advances the one and furnishes the other. Handling much material that will never attain the University, it should have, and, in its first class types it has, a certain completeness of its own. During the present experimental stage of our Universities, with so much that is inchoate and heterogenous, the College may well assert its own time-honored status, and refuse either to be diverted or misvalued. Our American fondness for novelty and bigness, for two-story fronts on one-story buildings, needs curbing rather than coddling, and the sincere and dutiful College should not be dazed or dazzled by the glamour of a polysyllable.

I do not speak of the lust for this top-title which has deluded some inferior schools, (not all of them in the West), schools whose actual product is sometimes not above that of a medium grade high-school, and whose intellectual frame is largely "front door and back yard."

A University, truly such, is a school where the science of subjects (and by implication many subjects) is explored to the utmost. In general the aim of the University is the subjects taught and the man as related to these: the aim of the College is the man taught and the subjects as related to him. President Seth Low puts it clearly in saying—"A College is conceived of as a place of liberal culture, a University as a place for specialization based upon liberal culture." The two functions should not be confused, nor either disparaged. They are in different tiers and to compound them is an awkward compromise. A given corporation may change from one to the other, but not by a mere change of title, only by an inward change of scope and emphasis and method.

Our American Universities are now, most of them, in transition. Their evolution is adolescent and incomplete. Harvard is feeling her way along a process of elimination. Her discussion of the reduction of her A. B. courses is one step in her palingenesis. She may take the full step now or later. She will take it. Taking it she must logically and naturally go further. In purposing to be a University pure and simple she decomplicates herself from the College idea. Granting, as an outsider must, the definiteness of her aim, that it is rational and not capricious, it must be understood as a direct move toward final and complete Universityhood. But even were that not yet the avowed or the intended end of her diminution of A. B. work, it is the proper and inevitable end.

This must decrease that that may increase. The shrinkage must match the growth. Harvard began by translating her sub-University work in the terms of specialistic study. She is now proceeding toward what she therein elected.

She will be a great advanced school—"Fair Harvard", still:

but she will cease to be Harvard College. Such a displacement of the College purpose and function by the University purpose and function establishes nothing save its own fact. It proves preference, not superiority. We trust that Harvard will, when entirely and completely a University, continue that renown which she attained and in which she throve when entirely a College. This is her q. e. d.

There must be Universities and there must be Colleges. Let each school make its own election, consistently and completely, and do its chosen work. Let neither face two ways.

I claim the liberty to speak for one *College*—a College that believes in its own function as one to be magnified and maintained— appreciating and testifying the separateness of disciplinary instruction from that which is technical and professional. This is a work to be done, and the Colleges are to do it, without pretension or apology.

Their contribution is of a kind that is indispensable not only toward a generous broadening and basing of manhood, but also indispensable to give to those particular schools assembled in the Universities such material as they themselves cannot best prepare either in quality or in abundance. I say quality, advisedly and boldly, assured that the College course is best interpreted and illustrated in the College that stands independently, unnarrowed by the influence which, when it adjoins an elaborate University scheme works down to pervert even the course in Arts from its broad function into a mere specialization. The functions of the disciplines presupposed in the A. B. degree, and of the investigations leading to higher degrees are decidedly unlike. The processes have different conclusions. One should make iron into steel, the other make steel into tools.

Specialization *not* "based upon liberal culture" attempts to put a fine edge on pot-iron. The man who is but a specialist and has no general aptitude is absurdly narrow and is less capable even in his own sphere. No Cyclops is lovely. Polyphemus may crush Acis, but he never can win Galatea. The winning man must be a wide man. High wall exacts broad sub-structure, or it will topple. The world's available men must be trained to be alert, supple, adaptive—to have an intelligent appreciation of various realms,—to be well-begun in many things, that so they may each both select his own life-specialty and understand its important bearings. Synthetic men, who have minds and hearts for the *ensemble* of life are quite as needful to the world's weal as are expert partialists. *Per centum* of the population more of them are necessary. Success then to the course that aims to make its student great in one thing: but success also to the course that makes him good in many.

Specialism is so important that it needs to be defended from its own dangers. A minister who is only a theologian, a doctor who knows medicine and no more, a lawyer whose whole library wears sheepskin, a teacher who is only a pedant (not truly a *pedagog*, because he prefers books to boys), a speaker who is only a declaimer, a high magistrate who is only a politician,—all these are narrow and narrowing. They have edge without back-blade, and they are "by their means defeated of their ends." They are too 'hollow ground.' On the contrary, one who, with only a general training, attempts a specialist's tasks will prove an empiric, and not an expert.

The world wants men who have both temper and point. Both. Neither by itself. You do not make a lancet out of a brad, nor shave with a barrel hoop. Technical study if it is not balanced by wide interest tends toward a petulant and paltry conceit.

A large introduction to philosophy, history, literature, law; a speaking acquaintance with many sciences, physical and political; a good grounding in logic and ethics—such discipline both in its matter and its method opens wide the mind toward the large world of things and thoughts.

To know anything at all well one must know it as related

and horizoned. Elisha Gray the inventor of the tel-autograph told me of an interview with a recent product of a course in that present fad of tyros,—electrical engineering. " I suppose you know all about electricity," said Dr. Gray. " I ought to (was the reply of the youth of twenty-one) I've studied nothing else for three years." " Ah, (said the inventor) I've studied electricity forty years, and I feel that I know nothing about it!"

Specialism is to be forefended from pedantry by that earlier patient exercise and enlargement of many faculties which promotes both competency and modesty. At a period like ours—a period that calls for the ripest and readiest power, there is small occasion to undervalue and skip that which widens and matures the whole man. So the College, *in situ*, may well demur to have its demonstrated value assailed or patronized by the University *in transitu*. And yet the College has had, and has, its due time begrudged and its true calling deprecated by many coteries of supercilious technicists. But what sound regard, I ask, toward advanced courses and their high exactions is that which is willing to take half-puddled material, and thro a foreshortened disciplinary preparation to rush men into the laboratory and the *seminar?*

Poor pulp, poor paper—no matter how fancifully watermarked, highly-calendered, and daintily-packed. A youth of eighteen may be wet with a College course in two years: but he cannot be saturated in less than four. We know of men 'dropping out of College' and dropping into special courses: but let us be reminded that nothing ever drops *up!*

The best is none too good for the imperious exactions of a time that sifts and selects its instruments with impartial severity and that sends to the auction-room all 'seconds.'

Over-haste must spill itself halfway, and arrive empty. Men who graduate Sophomores are apt to remain such. One there was who, tho the world was dying for Him, waited, until He was thirty, to begin to save it, growing into that wisdom and stature which were His equipment for complete ministry and without which He would not begin.  First Nazareth, then Jerusalem.

However I may traverse the opinions of those who are so graciously following me, I must be permitted to say resolutely that I believe it to be a demonstrable error to attempt to combine College and University into one school.

As an Academy should not try to be a College, so a College should not try to be a University.

As a College is handicapped by trying to include an Academy, so a University is handicapped by trying to include a College.

The sphere, the atmosphere, the whole *esprit*, of each is, and should be, individual and distinct.

Undergraduate work takes a different material, or takes its material at an entirely different stage. Those surroundings are not the best which are half one thing and half another. Each demands a peculiar adaptation in the qualities of instructors and in their standards and methods. Confusion of these trammels and frustrates. The accent should not be a compromise. A University course ought to be absolutely elective, of course by groups. Electives should be the incidents of the course in arts. Neither the mental nor the moral disciplines of the two coincide. The College student is and should be half-boy, the candidates for A. M., or Ph. D., should be all man. Not two cases or three, to be sure, but the averages, give the demarcation.

So I say firmly that in my opinion (be it worth never so little) the College that is contained in a University is not the best kind of a College, and that the University which attempts to include undergraduate work is not the best kind of a University. It is a College that does not rightly honor its own specialty of discipline, or it is a University that has not yet gotten its growth. In either case something is forfeited, either in prematurity or immaturity.

Let none take umbrage at this, for I seek the relative and peculiar honor of each set of functions. They are coordinate parts of one full system, they are not parts of each other. Germany separates from her *gymnasia* her special schools of science and philosophy, and it is retrogressive and abnormal to combine them here.

The College knows what it is doing and needs to do. Its task is still imperative. Its distinctiveness is its distinction. The firm, honest, high-class College of today gives a product all its own, and which it need not be ashamed to compare with any of like degree. Criticism is its atmosphere, as investigation is the atmosphere of the advanced post-graduate realm. The University course is to be guaged by its permissions: but the College course by its exactions; not by what a few may get out of it, but by what the more part must get who conquer its schedule and attain its *imprimatur*.

As subsequent to College life, University work has its unimpeachable importance; as a substitute for that life it is a failure. That such substitution is a failure may be argued by comparing the ratio in efficient success, between those who take special degrees after a true College experience and those who take these without such experience. To say nothing of the moral callowness of boys plunged into the (for them) too absolute irresponsibility of University surroundings strictly such, there is not only the chance but the likelihood that they will develop spindling and thin. It is bad husbandry to let an orchard run to apples until it has for some years developed sturdy wood. Precocious fruit robs fibre and sacrifices the perennial for the transient. The ultimate should be more than the proximate, the enduring held higher than the extempore, and 'the long run' preferred to the short dash.

It is by an instinct that is an argument that the typical College is relatively rural. The University is naturally urban and even metropolitan. The country is not its normal place, and, on the other hand, a city is no place for a College.

Numbers and the *eclat* of boisterous crowds are no adequate test of what is best and most effluent in either case. Certainly the College should be compact and wieldy in order most surely to emphasize each particular man. Some of you will join me good-naturedly to remind any who need reminding that the quality of a home is not always to be estimated by the size and costliness of the house, and that some of the best products of the world are still hand-made.

It is high time to make more distinct and positive the claim of the College proper to a place and power not to be superseded. It is high time to resent and to resist the assumptions of educators in specialistic realms who so readily volunteer an advice which they are not most competent to give, and a dictation of theories which are vitiated or at least devitalized by failure to consider the strict College area and requirement. University ideals and tasks are after their own kind and give no warrant of special competency in the philosophy of College ideals and tasks. *Ne sutor ultra crepidam.*

When President Woolsey could write: "Had I my life to live over again, I would throw in my lot with one of the smaller Colleges, where I could have more influence in training mind and shaping character," there is surely something to exalt in that differentiation which makes of each student an individual problem,—yes, and demonstration. The prime duty of a College professor is the study of students.

The thoro College course keens the mind while it binds the hearts of those who share its romance and comradeship. In rubbing men well together it reduces snobbery while it educates mutual respect for whatever is sterling and brave. And here I say that attending recitations in College subjects and at College age, is not necessarily "going to College." For a class-room at the end of a trolley or a cable is not *College!* Campus and dormitory and table and prize contest and athletic-field and chapel,—the *collectivity* of these is an elemental part of real College days. These adjuncts to the curriculum make up that whole influence and momentum which nothing else is like. I appeal to your memories, who have heard me so kindly. That enduring spell "of woven paces and of waving hands" which we can neither forget nor renew, that mystical sentiment of youth changing to manhood, that tearful charm—a "gleam of irrecoverable gold,"—you whose hearts all this once subdued, can you analyze or appraise it? Would you exchange it for aught else?

As A. B. graduates, let us then urge the values of those disciplines which cultivate all powers so that they may be applied to any subject, which compact men for either the demands of ripened investigations, or for the shock and pressure of affairs, putting first the broad and sound, and putting afterward the exceptional.

We are to honor the breasts that nursed us by being thoro and all-around men toward every present demand in church and school and government and enterprise. We owe it to ourselves to be true men of letters, interested in the whole record, lengthwise and widthwise, of human feeling and action, remembering so that all real literature is a transcript of life, having concrete ends for the soul and forever. As humanists, to whom nothing that is is alien, we are bound in duty to think into our rational and voluntary lives the problems and the proofs the motives and the ideals that make life most worthy when most exacting. *Festina lente*—wise paradox to con and keep! Haste without hurry,—*grow* then *go*,—that is the true College idea. The man is primary, speed is secondary.

This is the true order in life, therefore in education.

## CORRECTIONS

Page 21, line 11; omit "a" before "man."
Page 34, line 22; read—conclave of human hearts.
Page 36, title lines; read—New England Society of New York City.
Page 57, line 13; read—men who are unwilling.
Page 123, put verses beginning at foot of page in quotation marks.
Page 130, line 33; meditative, was misspelled.
Page 151, last line but two; omit the first "having."
Page 164, line 5; "know" should be read, knows.
      line 12; inverted n in recognition.
      line 15; read t for "i" in but.
Page 170, last line but four; exaggeration, was misspelled.

---

This limited edition, of one thousand copies, of HAMILTON, LINCOLN, AND OTHER ADDRESSES, was printed, from type, at the Courier Press, Clinton, N. Y., March, 1896.

www.ingramcontent.com/pod-product-compliance
Lightning Source LLC
Chambersburg PA
CBHW020843160426
43192CB00007B/764